GET THE PRICE RIGHT
DEPLOY POWERFUL PRICING STRATEGIES ON YOUR SHELVES AND GROW PROFITABLY

Heather,

Looking forward working with you.

Sh
30/03/2016

SAHAJ KOTHARI

GET THE PRICE RIGHT: DEPLOY POWERFUL PRICING STRATEGIES ON YOUR SHELVES AND GROW PROFITABLY

First published in September 2015

Copyright © 2015 Sahaj Kothari

Author: Sahaj Kothari
Book edited by - Lisa Browning

ISBN-13: 978-1517137601
ISBN-10: 1517137608

The right of Sahaj Kothari to be identified as the author of this work has been asserted by him in accordance with the Copyright, Design and Patents Act 1988.

All rights reserved. No part of this work may be reproduced in any material form (including photocopying or storing in any medium by electronics means and whether or not transiently or incidentally to some other use of this publication) without the written permission of the copyright holder.

www.ensere.com
www.sahajkothari.com
www.getthepricerightbook.com

Disclaimer

The author asserts that he cannot be held liable or responsible for the outcomes of decisions the reader makes as a result of reading this book. The reader is wholly responsible for their actions and should seek relevant professional advice before making a decision that may affect their business and life.

Contents

Acknowledgements	vii
Foreword	ix
Chapter 1: Introduction to the World of Retail	1
Chapter 2: Get the Price Right Because It Matters	11
Chapter 3: OLD is Not GOLD Anymore	23
Chapter 4: Strategic - Pricing - Execution (SPE)™ Framework	31
Chapter 5: Organisational Goals	37
Chapter 6: Shopper Goals is Your Key to Positioning	53
Chapter 7: Pricing Excellence in Action	63
Chapter 8: Winning at the Moment of Truth	91
Chapter 9: With Great Pricing Power Come Great Responsibilities	109
About the Author	115

To my beloved daughter

Ayra

My inspiration - you are priceless!

Acknowledgements

To one day write a book was a childhood ambition of mine. A big thank you to Raymond Aaron - my mentor, for his inspiring words that influenced me to distillate my aspiration into its physical form.

I am grateful for the abundant love from by dear parents who believed in me long before I did so myself. Thank you to my brother, sister and sister-in-law for their support in everything I do. Thank you to my grandparents for their love and well wishes. Thank you to my loving in-laws for their everlasting blessings. Thank you to all extended family and friends, for the support system and comfort they provide. I am indebted to them for the happiness they provide, without which I wouldn't have been in a position to write this book.

The content of my book is conceived from my personal experiences – every person I have worked with has been my teacher. To Simon Launay, my friend and mentor, for igniting the entrepreneurial spirit in me. My work on pricing has been inspired by Simon's own work in this arena. To my fantastic team, Simon Blackburn, Lorenzo Rampin, Asya Arabadzhiyska, Joe Tanner and Ben Phillips with whom I have spent countless hours on projects, and who have stuck by me through thick and thin. My team has been instrumental in influencing the experiences that I am able to share with you today.

Thank you also to the various organizations that have entrusted me to work with them on various projects. These opportunities form the backbone of my book, and are my inspiration to address this much discussed and vital component – the price. A special thank you to Stewart Beale, Ruth Connolly, Antony Watson, Martin Attock, Vincent Plane, Stephen Greiff, Sam Akinluyi and Peter Neville for providing such fantastic opportunities.

A huge thank you to Chinmai Swamy the Branding sage and a good friend, for providing indispensable support towards the completion of my book. To Raveena Chordia, for her dedication and astounding support with the book cover. Thank you to my personal book architects, Vishal Morjaria and Naval Kumar, for keeping me on track to complete the book despite any hurdles. To my editor, Lisa Browning, for her essential edits and for making sense of my writing.

Lastly, a special thank you to my wife, Anisha, for her encouragement, love, and support during the many months it took me to write this book. She has been instrumental in providing invaluable feedback on my writing and shaping this book into the correct form for my readers. I would not have been able to do this without you.

Foreword

The global retail environment today is evolving at a rapid rate. Shoppers have become savvier and more sophisticated, while organisations (retailers and manufacturers) are scrambling to innovate and battling just to stay in the game. Businesses are currently struggling with numerous price cuts and fierce competition in-store. As they say, sustaining being 'flat' is the new 'growth' for most organisations. The current situation appears to be just the beginning and is projected to deteriorate. The question now facing us is whether there is a sustainable path ahead for everyone.

Price is currently the most talked about topic in the retail industry and, in this book, Sahaj provides a pragmatic and end-to-end approach to getting it right – from strategy to execution, regardless of the market conditions. Sahaj has put together a compelling solution contained in his Strategic Pricing Execution (SPE) ™ framework. He demonstrates a very strong vision for organisations to not just GROW but to GROW profitability in a manner that results in a win-win situation with the shoppers of today. The SPE™ framework uses vocabulary that is easy to understand within the organisations, and introduces concepts that are simplified and grounded in the realities of today.

Sahaj is committed to making retail a better place for all, and GET THE PRICE RIGHT is truly the first dedicated book on the subject of retail pricing. It is the most practical guide on retail pricing for the 21st century. It gives marketing, sales and finance managers and leaders simple, achievable pricing strategies that will deliver sustainable growth. Can you afford to leave money on the table? If not, GET THE PRICE RIGHT is the guide for you.

Raymond Aaron
New York Times Top 10 Best-Selling Author

Chapter 1
Introduction to the World of Retail

"Any customer can have a car painted any colour that he wants so long as it is black."
- Henry Ford, about the "Model T" in 1909

There is much debate about how serious Henry Ford was when he made that remark about the Model T, but this statement could reflect a retailers dream – being able to dictate shopper preferences.

Unfortunately for today's retailers, the reality is in stark contrast. The current global retail environment can be considered to be hostile in comparison. We are in a new era that is increasingly being shaped by technological advances, globalisation and a volatile economic environment. The term 'different' is a very mild one when comparing shoppers in today's retail environment with those from ten years ago.

Price has been a key growth factor influencing businesses for centuries. Over the last decade, we have observed an exponential growth in its utilisation and application as a strategic tool in retail. Even the best products and brands face the threat of commoditisation in today's fiercely competitive markets – at both the global and local level.

Manage to get your price effectively, and you will see your organisation grow profitably. However, if you fail, or even worse, manage price incorrectly, all you can do is hope. This then becomes a gamble, and we all know who wins in the casino – and it's not us.

What is Price?

The Oxford dictionary defines price as "the amount of money expected, required or given in payment for something'.

Price is a term that the majority of people use, and claim to understand well. In my experience, price is like an iceberg. Most people believe that they have seen all there is to pricing, until they are exposed to the real reach of its impact. In my opinion the above definition is very simplistic in nature, and does not showcase the true power and potential one has with getting your price right.

Price is a critical factor influencing the GROWTH and PROFITABILITY of every organisation. Yet, the majority of us rely on a few traditional techniques that are no longer effective.

The Retail Conundrum - the chaos today

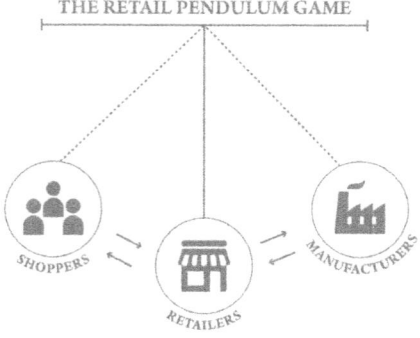

Figure 1.1: The retail pendulum

The Shopper

Imagine going out shopping one fine evening; walking into a supermarket store for your weekly grocery shop or a retail store for that clothing item you have wanted to purchase for some time now. Ever wondered why, nine out of ten times, you leave the store either having bought more than you intended to or buying something that was not even on your shopping list in the first place?

The surprising fact is that the majority of us do not even realise when this happens. This series of events is not just random luck on part of the retailers – it is by careful design. Whether you happen to stumble across a lucrative 'limited edition' promotion, or find yourself perusing a store aisle you did not originally intend to, all of this is designed to achieve a singular objective – to sell to you, the shopper, at any cost. When you, as the shopper, realise that the same 'limited' promotion is still available six months on at the same retail store, that might spark a degree of disappointment. Is there a way out for the shoppers?

The Retailer

Retailers see promotions as a necessary evil. Ideally, they would love to have shoppers purchase their products at full price at any given time, but with the intensifying competition, they are fighting for market share at the expense of profit.

The shoppers of today are a stark contrast to those from a decade ago. With the consequence of the recent global recession and the ever-growing influence of technology in today's information age, shoppers have been trained and conditioned to become deal seekers. As a result, every retailer's marketing and in-store promotional campaign is dictated by the notion that

'Price is king'. This is costing retailers substantial expenditure to remain on the playing field. The switching rate of shoppers between retailers is at its peak, and there are no signs of it stabilising any time soon. These tough market conditions are compelling certain retailers to engage in dirty pricing tactics with the shoppers. Is there a way out for the retailers?

The Manufacturer

Manufacturers (or suppliers) have not been left out of this challenging maze. Retailers inevitably pass the cost of pricing back on to their suppliers who, on most occasions, end up funding the majority of the in-store promotions. Manufacturers are pressured into supporting retailers by providing them with a differentiated product offer at the best possible price. The bigger the retailer is, the higher its demands. And with increasing demands, the supplier's supply chain complexity has reached an all-time high while profit growth is at an all-time low. Is there a way out for the manufacturers?

The Retail Conundrum

As a result of these challenges, the retail environment is essentially composed of tactical plays, wherein short-term unsustainable gains override the longer-term sustainable growth aspirations. If the current trend endures, each participant's frustration will continue to rise, with the possibility of some manufacturers and retailers, especially those operating on a smaller scale, going out of business or facing acquisition by a stronger organisation.

The majority of retailers and manufacturers are leveraging price tactics for survival instead of driving growth in its true sense. If this were a game, the rules have changed from what they used to be a decade earlier. In fact, most of the 'players' (retailers, manufacturers), 'referees' (retail governing associations) and even 'audiences' (shoppers) have evolved in the way they interact with each other. So shouldn't we change our tactics to play and win the retail game? If they don't keep up with the race, the stakes are too high.

There is a way out for all

I have spent the last decade exploring and studying the ins and outs of the retail industry, experiencing it from the perspective of the shopper, consumer, retailer and manufacturer. This has enabled me to comprehend and influence the retail environment with a balanced approach in order to assist organisations of varying sizes in shaping and revamping their pricing strategies and tactics for GROWTH.

I have reviewed and adapted my techniques to align with the changing dynamics of the market, and they work. Some of these are simple and pragmatic commercial solutions, while others can be identified as being a little more scientific, tapping into human psychology and behaviour.

Why retail pricing deserves its own space and attention

The retail environment has unique attributes in comparison to that of other industries, specifically on the physical front. When you enter a retail store, there are pre-defined products and price offers set out for the shoppers. As a shopper you do not have the ability of bargaining for a better deal– you either take it or leave it. As a retailer, you usually do not offer different prices for different shoppers for the same product.

The retailer has to clearly display prices on the shelves in advance; you do not have the opportunity to market the benefits of the products before offering the customer a price based on the specific shopper's budget / disposable income. Retailers are currently unable to customise their marketing message to target individual shoppers at point of retail. Every shopper entering the retail store will be presented with the same buying opportunity – the same products with the same marketing message at the same price is offered on the shelves.

As a manufacturer, your products will be placed next to that of your competitors'. There are usually no sales personnel present to directly influence the shopper to purchase your product over others, or to provide customers with extra incentives at the point of purchase.

These attributes, specific to the retail environment, clearly outline some of the challenges and constraints of getting your price right for the products on the shelves, and therefore require a targeted approach for achieving this.

Why did I write this book?

So what was my motivation to write this book? Firstly, I wanted to share my experience and contribute towards the progress of the future retail environment. The current trend in retail pricing is unsustainable, and if the industry continues on the same path, it is inevitable that certain retailers and manufacturers will go out of business, be acquired or be forced to change the core of their business model. However I have a vision to make the Retail experience more refreshing, engaging and progressive, and I want to do my part.

I also want to raise awareness of some faulty practices currently being applied within the industry, and provide pragmatic solutions to some of the toughest challenges. My solutions work, and I want to share them with you. My objective here is NOT to share every single bit of information on retail pricing. That's boring, that's transactional, and it would just be theoretical. Instead, my ambition is to distil a few CORE principles THAT MATTER, THAT RESONATE and that will give you RESULTS if you implement them well.

Secondly, I was unable to locate a credible book focused on the pricing of products on shelves. While there are innumerable publications on general pricing strategies and tactics, none of them focused on the retail industry specifically. One can find lots of opinions on this topic in smaller chunks, in the form of blogs and articles, but the majority of these only address part of the story. I wanted to compile and present a holistic viewpoint on the current hot topic of the retail industry.

Who should read this book and why?

This book has been written for anyone who is involved in influencing and determining the retail price. When I refer to the retail sector, I am referring to both high street retailers and supermarkets. As a guide this book will benefit individuals at all levels in the sales, marketing, finance and procurement teams within the retailers' and manufacturers' organisations.

As much as the book primarily refers to retail, the majority of the recommended applications can be easily adapted to any other industry – both private and public, irrespective of size. I have personally applied a number of these pricing principles to significantly drive profitable growth for organisations within the telecommunication, entertainment & media, powers & utilities and government sectors.

Every business is different, and you will find that some of the applications are more relevant to your individual requirements than others. Therefore, I encourage you to keep an open and explorative mind when considering cross-industry applications.

The book is a collection of key observations of what actually works in the marketplace, and does not simply espouse theoretical jargon. I want to encourage you to consider how each of the strategies outlined is relevant to your business, and in what shape would you could implement it within your organisation.

GET THE PRICE RIGHT is the only practical guide focused on pricing in the new retail era. Can you afford to leave money on the table? If not, GET THE PRICE RIGHT is the guide for you.

Structure of the book

This book introduces my three-stage Strategic-Pricing-Execution (SPE) ™ framework, which has been designed to address the pricing challenges of today's retail industry using a balanced approach. Chapters 2 and 3 provide the context and set the foundations for the subsequent chapters. Chapter 4 outlines the 3 stage (SPE) ™ framework in further detail. Stage 1, which is discussed in Chapters 5 and 6, establishes the correct strategic course for your pricing strategy. Stage 2 (in Chapter 7) outlines key principles and tactics at your disposal for devising pricing strategy and plan. Stage 3 (in Chapter 8) links the pricing principles and plan into a coherent in-store execution. This end-to-end approach is a MUST for any business wanting to get their price right.

I understand it will take more than just price to get things in order, but based on my experience and that of other industry experts, price is a significant focus point and challenge within the industry, and is usually a good place to start.

FREE Bonuses

I want to give the readers with more than just a good read. There are limitations to what I can include in the book. To further assist and add to your tool-kit, you can find more supporting material to download on the book's website, www.GetThePriceRight.com, for FREE. These include additional informative illustrations, example case studies, model templates and more.

I would personally love to hear from you. Please do visit the site and send me your thoughts on the book. Tell me what resonated the most with you. Share your own stories on how you have used creative pricing strategies in your organisations. What did you find to be the most difficult thing? The best examples will be promoted on the site, and if you like, can be cited as case studies in the future editions of this book. Together let's make retail a better place for retailers, manufacturers and shoppers.

Chapter 2
Get the Price Right Because It Matters

"Nowadays people know the price of everything and the value of nothing."
- Oscar Wilde, The Pictures of Dorian Gray

Oscar Wilde's quote applies perfectly to the majority of organisations. Their understanding of price and perception of value span a great divide as most organisations still rely on their legacy systems when it comes to making pricing decisions.

Why should you care about Pricing?

Price is a key determinant in the shopper's decision-making process for purchasing a product, and can influence the growth or survival of an organisation. Both a price that is too high and one that is too low can limit growth.

It is important to clarify that the price that we are referring to is the retail price – the price that shoppers pay at the till to purchase the product. These can be divided into two categories – base price and promo price. Base price is an everyday (higher) price and promo price is the special price discount that the shoppers receive on the base price. Some retailers follow the strategy of every day lower price (EDLP) – which simply means one standard price 365 days a week across the product range.

For retailers, price is currently one of the strongest levers within their marketing toolkit to drive shopper footfall into their stores. Every retailer claims to have the lowest price, providing the lowest basket spend for their shoppers, or else they offer to pay back the difference (at the next store visit). The emphasis is dominantly on price. Even if a retailer talks about giving 'value', the subliminal messages within it will still put more emphasis on price (or savings) than on any other feature.

Figure 2.1: Price is a prominent feature of a product on the shelf

In the above example, what do you see? What do you feel? Would it be fair to say that price was a fundamental element in your thought and emotional equation? The majority of the time, price is the first or the second feature of the product that the shopper sees and considers – either consciously or subconsciously. Prices are bluntly showcased across the retail floor, especially when there is a discount available. Shoppers can compare products from various manufacturers within a few seconds, and price is usually the key component of that judgment.

If you think I have chosen a product type with limited physical differences, I have uploaded additional examples on the website www.GetThePriceRight.com. Evaluate them yourself and let me know what you think. The results will be very similar, if not the same.

Price is the key element of the INTERNAL profit equation

There have been countless illustrations emphasising the impact on profit due to x% price increase, which is equivalent to a higher number of y% cost reduction initiatives i.e. a small price increase has a large impact on your bottom line profit. One famous study on this topic was conducted by McKinsey, who published an article claiming that 'A price rise of 1% at an average company in the S&P 1500 index, which includes large, medium and small cap companies, would generate an 8% increase in operating profit if volumes remain steady - an impact nearly 50% greater than that of a 1 percent fall in variable costs such as materials and direct labor and more than 300% greater than the impact of a 1 percent increase in volume.'

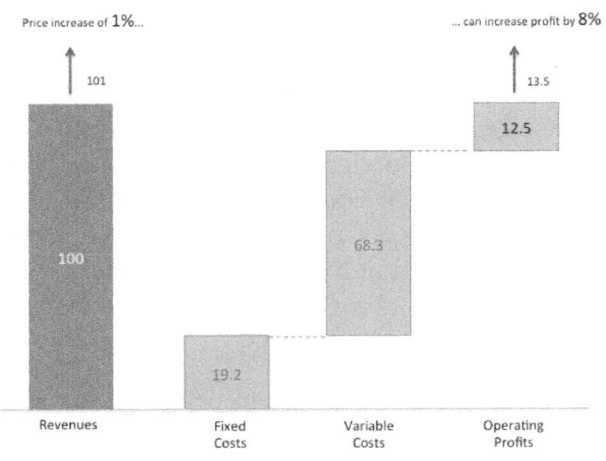

Figure 2.2: The power of one (For demonstration purpose only)

The idea is a very simple one, and theoretically true based on the simple math on revenue and profit equations. Do I agree with it? Maybe, is my response. I believe that price can have a significant impact on the profit equation, and this analysis helps managers to consider pricing more seriously (than cost cutting exercises) and with much more rigor than many may normally do. However, the retail environment is far from what is encapsulated within this illustration, and one should be cautious of relying on such statistics.

Price increases are likely to have a detrimental impact on your volumes, to the extent that certain price increases can actually hurt your overall revenue and profit. This could be true for products with a high price elasticity factor (i.e. those more sensitive to price) or when crossing certain sensitive price thresholds. For such products, it is important to understand what happens to the lost volume due to price increases. Is it absorbed into your own product portfolio, or is it lost to your competitors, or has the shopper just stopped buying the product?

It is important to view these scenarios at the portfolio level instead of just on a product-by-product basis. We will further explore how we can access our portfolio in Chapter 5, and share alternative solutions to dealing with products with higher elasticity (in Chapter 7). For now, I just wanted to share that although retail pricing is not straightforward, despite such challenges, there is light at the end of the tunnel.

Invoice pricing can be complicated

For manufacturers, in regards to pricing, their core focus is to get their invoice prices right. This is the price that they charge retailers for their products. The concept is relatively simple, however the real pricing story goes beyond that.

"Don't see your new product for $21. Offer it at $1,000,021 with a rebate of $1,000,000. People will think it's a great bargain when in fact its just a huge inconvenience. All we need is one person to forget to mail in the rebate forms." Mr. Anomalous

The true depth of this topic of invoice pricing goes beyond the scope of the book, but I want to touch on it briefly to emphasise the sheer practical complexity that exists between the retailer and the manufacturer.

Over the past decade, manufacturers have tried to entice retail buyers with a growing number of offline discounts. Such discounts can include discounts for online orders, bulk-buying discounts, performance based discounts, discounts for being 'strategic and collaborative' partners, and more. These discounts are costs to the manufacturers and extra profits for the retailers, and are often not included on the invoice. In another scenario, where a retail price increase is shortly followed by an increase in promotion discounts offered by manufacturers, it further complicates the ability to truly understand the impact of pricing on the profit margin.

Value Equation for the Shoppers

Retailers and manufacturers can undertake varied research and analyses in advance, but the effectiveness of their plans and actions boils down to whether the shopper will respond positively or not at the moment of truth - the retail store. Will the shopper pick up and buy their products from the shelves?

This section introduces the shopper's decision-making framework and principles, which form the key foundation for other chapters. Chapter 6 further develops this concept and articulates the practical approach we can take in positioning our pricing strategies.

Shoppers make their decision based not on fair price, but fair value (perceived benefits minus actual price). This concept is a widely accepted one, stating that we should focus on the value we provide to our shoppers. The shoppers assess the value of the products from various manufacturers, and essentially determine whether the value to them of buying the product is equal to or greater than the price they are being asked to pay.

On a more basic level, every emotion can be divided into two types – it can either be a good emotion or a bad emotion. A good emotion drives pleasure, while a bad emotion drives pain. The net worth of the value equation can be thought of as the perceived pleasure (benefits) one receives from the product minus the perceived pain (the price). You occasionally hear the statement that price was the reason we did not make that sale. In fact what they are actually referring to is the net value of the product being the key reason.

Figure 2.3 depicts the balancing scale of the value equation:

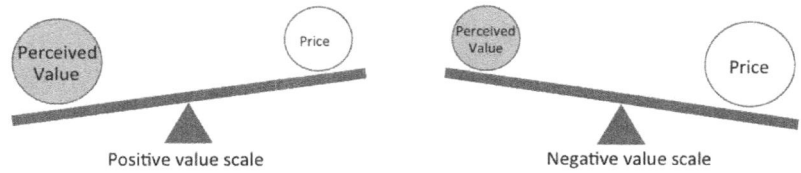

Positive value scale   Negative value scale

Figure 2.3: Net Value Scale

Note that this equation has zero reference to the actual cost of producing and delivering the product for the retailers or manufacturers. The majority of organisations are so fixated with getting the right financial numbers that they either undermine or lose the whole premise of the existence of the product in the first place. Lack of product excitement and innovation increases the pressure on price cuts. A strong brand and product feature injects good emotions, and can help increase perceived value.

If price is considered to be a painful emotion, why do retailers' marketing campaigns revolve primarily around PRICE? In the midst of such a competitive market, majority of the retailers have failed to raise the bar of perceived value for their shoppers, and therefore have reverted to the tactic of reducing pain by indulging in competitive prices and promotions.

Perceived value is a long-term gain, while price can be used for short-term gains. Retailers understand this trend and have come to realize that this is not a recession specific phenomenon. We may be out of the recession now, but shopper attitudes have not reverted to what they were earlier. As a result, we have indirectly conditioned the shopper to think that price is more important than value in their decision-making process. The retailer's pain is the shopper's pleasure and vice versa. By focusing on price to reduce pain for the shopper, you are reducing pleasure for the retailer! This is surely unsustainable in the longer run.

Psychology of decision making for the shoppers

The concept of pleasure versus pain is a simple one, but how does a shopper actually calibrate their value scale? Perception is very subjective; how do shoppers identify the product as being high or low on their own personal value scale? If a shopper decides to purchase the product from the shelves, is it an instantaneous decision or is it a result of an internal pro and con debate within them?

I found my answers with Daniel Kahneman's explanation of how decisions are influenced through psychological processes. In 2002 Daniel Kahneman won the Nobel Prize for Economics – the first psychologist to ever achieve this, bridging experimental psychology and behavioural economics. He articulated a system for our behaviour and decision-making process. It revealed explanations for how shoppers perceive pricing signals and how price really fits into their decision-making equation.

Kahneman's decision-making framework for humans has two distinct mental processes that he calls systems – 'System 1' and 'System 2'. System 1 integrates perception and intuition. It's lazy, switched on 24-7, associative, run on autopilot with limited control, without any effort, very fast, and for slow learning. In comparison, System 2 is slow, effortful and hence energy hungry, logical in process, but is more flexible and controllable. In simple terms, System 1 is our intuition engine, which relies on our experiences. It is mostly associated with our everyday tasks and highly skilled mental activities. System 2 is our thinking engine for making deliberate decisions, which relies on logical facts.

For further references, you can find illustrations of the Kahneman's decision-making framework on www.GetThePriceRightBook.com.

Kahneman's concept triggered a transformational change in my perception of what pricing really is. Does price trigger System 1 or System 2 for the shopper? It is different for different shoppers. If the shoppers have been conditioned over time to expect what they get from the product at a consistent price, then System 1 would kick in as long as they need the product. However, a material change of any sort is likely to trigger System 2.

Get the Price Right

For example, a small re-engineering of the product, such as reducing the weight of a can of soft drink from 330ml to 300ml while keeping the price the same, is likely to be governed by System 2. The original 330ml can, or even potentially a competing product sitting next to it on the retail shelf, acts as a reference point. The logical mind would interpret this as an approximate decrease of 10% in the product for the same price. The shopper's mind would then consciously or subconsciously engage in deciding if it is still a fair price. On the contrary, ensuring that the new product packaging is designed to minimise any variation in the physical appearance of weight-out could potentially keep the shopper on auto-purchase under System 1. The shopper may not even realise the change, or would consider the change as being immaterial.

If a manufacturer decides to launch a brand new product, they have the opportunity to guide the shopper in the manner they desire. Shoppers have not formed any direct association with the product to begin with, but that does not limit them in making any judgement calls, even on day one of the product's launch, on what would be a fair price. In the absence of direct association, based on the attributes of the product, System 1 will instantaneously direct the shoppers to their next best associative experience for reference. This could be based on their personal experience and circumstance, such as their preferences and disposable income. Possessing a strong brand provides a significant advantage in keeping the shoppers on auto-purchase as per System 1 regardless of what the product may be. If System 1 fails to convince the shopper to purchase your products, their mental process switches to System 2 for answers. The logical step with System 2 would be to then compare the new product with other competing products available next to it on the shelves. The place where your product is showcased in the store can significantly influence the shopper's mental reference point for price. This therefore demands an absolute knowledge of your shoppers' requirements and formulating your desired price positioning accurately.

Psychology is one of the main influences on successful pricing. Chapters 6 - 8 further develop this concept and articulate the practical approach we can take in positioning our pricing strategies.

Consistent pricing is your survival kit in difficult markets

We realise the importance of price, but does everyone in the organisation view it from the same lens? No they do not. From the simplified viewpoint of the manufacturer, price is important to marketers because it represents the marketers' assessment of the value customers see in the product or service, and what the shopper is willing to pay for it. For the sales team, price is a key negotiating weapon with their customers to get the best possible deal, which enables them to achieve their periodic targets. For the finance team, while product and place (of the 4Ps) affect costs, pricing is the only element that directly affects revenues and thus profit.

If products were not performing well in the market, the sales team would partly lay blame on the marketers for lacking a strong brand presence and competitive edge. The finance team would blame the sales team for providing extensive promotions in-store to gain volume share at the expense of profit margins. Marketers could blame a lack of resources to make their dream product a reality. Some organisations are better than others, but the lack of congruence with the overall strategic ambitions, including pricing strategies, is one of the critical causes of reactive decision-making for manufacturers and therefore retailers. Chapter 5 is the starting step in ensuring that everyone is on the same page.

Get the Price Right

Getting your price right is one thing, but it is equally important to understand and align the reasons behind the pricing decision across the organisation. This can be the difference between success and failure when the market conditions are demanding. Unaligned strategies will drive reactive and chaotic actions by the retailers and manufacturers, with the primary purpose of survival. Have consistency in your communication – do you want to focus on increasing pleasure or reducing pain for the shoppers, and how would you like to do it?

If you want to increase pleasure for future sustainability, but your marketing messages revolve around price, then your shoppers will get mixed messages. In this case, if you are unable to provide a concise and consistent message regarding your product's features, shoppers will have no choice but to focus on price, the emotion of pain. Do it right, and do it consistently.

I have now shared with you two simple yet powerful frameworks for influencing pricing – value equation pricing and Kahneman's decision-making framework. These will become the foundations for understanding key pricing strategies and tactics in the following chapters.

Chapter 3
OLD Is Not GOLD Anymore

"If you want something you've never had, you must be willing to do something you've never done."
- Thomas Jefferson

History is testament to the power of change – evolution is an ideal example with its theory of survival of the fittest. Similarly, in the market place, agile organisations that are able to quickly adapt to meet challenges from competition, the economic environment and technological advances are able to come out on top. If you desire different results to what you have had so far, it is important to take lessons learnt from history and do it differently going forward.

Individuals within the organisation who influences pricing decisions can take many forms and can have a very diverse set of objectives. The right price needs to ensure that brand equity is maintained or enhanced, that transactions are profitable, competitive in nature, sustainable in the longer run and most importantly, help the shopper in their value equation. Developing a pricing strategy in equilibrium with all of this is almost impossible in any given situation. One can aspire to achieve these, but the harsh reality of the market is to focus on a few of these elements that are relevant to your situation.

Having worked with numerous businesses across various industries over the years, I have found that very few organisations give price the right level of focus and attention within their operations. A few organisations were on top of their game and some had great aspirations but lacked the right execution tactics, but the majority of them adopted the same pricing strategies they used 20 years ago. I may appear to be exaggerating here, but the reality is not that different. Many organisations are running on an autopilot of their legacy of doing things, and it is no wonder pricing has not been leveraged well for them.

This chapter considers some of these legacy approaches to pricing, and some of the challenges associated with it in today's market.

Matching or undercutting competitors on price

This a popular pricing method adopted by both retailers and manufacturers. Pricing in the retail environment has always been transparent, but with increasing advances in technology, shoppers are able to compare prices of any product with just a few clicks online, without even leaving the comfort of their homes. The combination of global recession and technological advances has conditioned shoppers to engage in comparison shopping before making their purchasing decision in favour of the product providing them with the best value. This still does not necessarily have to be the cheapest in the market. With the majority of retailers placing an increasing emphasis on 'being the cheapest', shoppers have been trained to believe that providing the cheapest price is the same as providing 'value'. In the midst of this, it is even more important to focus on the value delivered to the customer, drive innovation and be creative in your pricing strategies to remain ahead of the race.

The fundamental concern with matching or undercutting price tactics is that there can always be another business able to further undercut your price. Only large organisations, with

Get the Price Right

significant economies of scale and/or without any significant competitor(s), will be able to sustain this practice - and that too, only for a short period of time. This can only be a successful campaign for winning a short-term battle, but not the price war.

Price has the power to position your brand. Reflecting back on System 1 and 2 of our mental process framework (as outlined in Chapter 2), focusing on price will trigger System 2 of the shopper's mind-set, engaging in logical reasoning to convince themselves to purchase your product. If you are fighting the price war untactfully, the shopper is forced to place significant thought on price, with limited focus on other characteristics of the products, and will therefore most likely decide on the cheapest offering.

A lot of this is deceptive. A number of supermarkets run their marketing campaigns on being 'the cheapest in the market or they will refund the difference to the shopper on their next purchase'. How realistic is this? Take a note of the specifics of what they are offering– they compare each shopper's basket cost rather than cost per product. The approach of cost per basket is likely to balance out the net difference between the retailers of promoted and non-promoted products. Yes, shoppers may get some money back, but not to the extent that it appears. As a shopper, if you want to recoup the maximum benefit from the offer, the next time you are shopping for groceries, split your basket into products under promotions and those at full price and purchase them separately. You are likely to gain an overall higher cash sum back as difference. Try it before the retailers change their tactics yet again!

Assessing your competitors is the right move, but organisations fail to maximise their opportunity when they prioritise competitor risks ahead of their own organisational priorities or focus on the value to the shoppers. Undercutting competitors may help you gain short-term market share, but your growth is achieved at the expense of your profits - this is unsustainable.

There are ways to avoid market locking at certain price points, and these will be further examined in Chapter 7.

Cost based pricing

One of the most common pricing methods adopted by organisations, and this is also the one with the highest number of flaws in truly understanding the purpose of pricing. In fact, this is the most common pricing technique adopted across businesses globally. This is when an organisation calculates its true cost and adds on a 'reasonable' mark-up as profit (e.g. 10%, 20%) to define their pricing. There are a few variations of this approach, but all have similar flaws.

Does this approach have any consideration of the product's value to the shopper or does it attempt to incorporate the psychology of the shopper in their pricing? No, it is an inward-looking approach that is not balanced in its very nature. If all you are focusing on is the cost element of the product, what are the underlying messages that you are trying to communicate to your shoppers? Is it that you can source the raw materials at a much cheaper rate than what the shoppers could do? Is it that you can 'assemble' the raw materials in a more cost-effective way than what shoppers can do? Imagine shoppers standing in front of a potato snack aisle in the store. Would they be thinking about the sourcing of the potatoes and how effectively they were cooked? Hmm... Not really!

Cost is an important factor, but it is only a small part of the pricing equation. At most, it helps you to understand the lowest price you should charge your shoppers – your pricing 'floor'.

Even this may only be a subjective view, as the true cost per product is dependent on the volume you produce and sell. Cost has two components – the fixed cost (which does not change with volume, like machinery) and the variable cost (the incremental cost per product). The higher the sell volume rate, the lower the average fixed cost per product. Establishing a true cost per product is dependent on a fairly good estimate of how much you are going to sell.

Cost plus profit simply does not give the shoppers any compelling reason to buy, and you may be foregoing a significant opportunity in doing so.

Cyclical inflation based pricing - Pass on the inflation burden on to your shoppers

Some organisations have a pricing policy that simply involves raising your prices in line with your inflation or the standard national inflation rate. The latter option appears to be easier on the face value in convincing retailers (in the case of manufacturers) or shoppers (in case of retailers) that they have no role in pricing and that it is a direct result of challenging market conditions. Cost price increase for manufacturers is a regular topic of discussion with their counterparts in the retail industry.

Manufacturers often have distinct reasons driving their price increase recommendations. For example, the cost of raw materials may be increasing, and they would like to recoup all or part of this by passing it on to their customers (i.e. the retailers) by increasing the prices on the relevant products. However sometimes the reasoning is not that forthright, and they may be masked by some obscure and incomplete facts that are used to create a compelling shopper and customer 'story'. On the other hand, no such debate takes place between the retailer and the shoppers. Shoppers either accept or reject the new price increase by purchasing the product or not. This is their way of providing feedback to the retailers and the manufacturers.

Whether you consider the practice of inflationary based price increase to be complex or simple, this is still an internal view and is rooted in only making the numbers on the paper look good, i.e. let's not absorb the hit on our profit numbers due to increasing cost of goods. If the inflation levels are negligible, there is a possibility that shoppers may not notice.

The underlying problems are similar to that of the approaches discussed earlier, cost plus pricing and battling with competitors on pricing. None of these links to the value delivered to the shoppers. This becomes a transactional activity instead of being a strategic intervention in positioning your product in the correct position in the marketplace.

Conclusion

These are some of the widespread, entrenched approaches to pricing that do not require much imagination. I have not even mentioned the instances where the pricing decision is a result of guesswork of a few individuals within the organisation. I am not talking about random guesses – these decisions are based on instincts, experience and educated guesses. I have witnessed situations where a senior member of the organisation quotes a price figure based on an educated guess, which is then shared across the organisation as obvious facts. There you go – your pricing has been done in few seconds. One should be wary of such organisational culture and ways of working.

Overall, none of these approaches utilise an understanding of the perceived value to the shopper, or the price the shopper is willing to pay for your products. If you do not have answers to such questions aligned across the organisation, surely when the going gets tough in the market, price cuts may be an easy but usually the wrong option on the table. Your pricing decision requires a degree of forethought, analytics and research that only the best organisations invest in. If you have similar pricing challenges within your organisation, I would love to hear from you. Share your success stories or challenges with me on www.GetThePriceRightbook.com.

Chapter 4
Strategic - Pricing - Execution (SPE) ™ Framework

*"You have many habits that weaken you.
The secret of change is to focus all of your energy,
not on fighting the old, but on building the new."*
- Dan Millman, 'Way of the Peaceful Warrior', 1980

As discussed in the previous chapter, there are a number of concepts that have historically been used by organisations to formulate the price for their products. We also know that these techniques create a tunnel vision wherein the organizational objectives, strategic direction, and market demands may not be taken into account. I have created the Strategic-Pricing-Execution (SPE) TM Framework to bring a more comprehensive and coherent solution to creating a pricing strategy that outlines a clear role and purpose of pricing and syncs the process from conception to execution.

Avoid imbalance within your organisation

The organisation as a whole is responsible for the pricing decision, and should not be left for a few players to formulate it in isolation. Getting your price right can be the difference between sustainable profitable growth and fighting for survival in the market. Very few organisations give it the priority it duly deserves. The majority of organisations blame the market conditions for limiting their influence in shaping their price for positive growth. However every major organisation has been influential in getting the market to this very competitive point in the first place. This is true for challenger brands as well. It might be true that the market is in a very difficult place right now, but it is just responding to the decisions and actions you have taken a few years back. If you are asked what the organisation could have done many years ago to avoid the challenging scenario we are in today, you and your team can easily come up with reasonable set of potential solutions.

Having worked with multiple organisations in assisting them with their growth and pricing strategies, I have realised that these challenges are usually driven by 3 key factors. All of these factors create an imbalance within the organisation and in its subsequent actions. These 3 factors are:

1. An imbalance of power within the organisation teams,
2. An imbalance of focus between short-term actions versus longer-term aspirations, and
3. An imbalance between strategy, plan and execution

Currently, retailers and manufacturers have adopted a reactive stance to their market elements. I have constantly observed a discord between the objectives of the finance, marketing and sales teams – one team is focussed driving brand equity and positioning over a longer time period, while the other is keen to close the deal and drive the sales number for the month. One focuses on internal financials or supply chain management, while others on the needs of the shoppers from an external point of view, and so on. So, who wins? It truly depends on the leadership and the culture of the organisation that defines the level of priority for each initiative.

One of our clients (before we joined forces) had gone through a transformational change from being a category driving force to fighting for survival within a span of just 5 years.

Get the Price Right

What went wrong? In my opinion the balance of power between different functions within the organisation became skewed as the establishment of a new leadership structure gave sales team unbiased attention and power. I am not laying blame on the sales team for this drastic demise of the brand, but highlighting the consequence of the imbalance between the different functional teams.

SPE™ is the answer

My Strategic-Pricing-Execution (SPE) ™ framework was developed to tackle challenges of imbalance organisations and complex market dynamics. The approach is based on my personal experience of helping several organisations in getting the price right, and have filtered what works and what doesn't in the real world.

"As a Branding Coach myself I know how important it is to get the price right, the SPE™ will definitely help you to make your tactical decision right the first time and start emptying your shelves. Highly recommend it." Chinmai Swamy, The Branding Coach and the creator of The Brand Marketing Academy

SPE, as the name suggests, has 3 stages as shown in figure 4.1

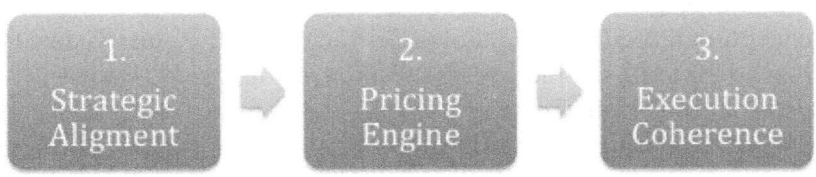

Figure 4.1: Three stages of the SPE ™ framework

- Stage 1 is the process of setting the right direction for your pricing strategy (covered in chapter 5 and 6)
- Stage 2 outlines key principles and tactics you can adopt for building your pricing plan (covered in chapter 7)
- Stage 3 is to link transform the pricing plan into coherent in-store execution tactics (covered in chapter 8)

This end-to-end approach is a necessity for anyone wanting to get their price right.

Without establishing a strategic goal post, competitive market conditions may force organisations to take drastic actions with a short-term focus. As you may be losing shoppers to your competitors, such actions are usually reactive in. Therefore Stage 1 is a critical step before diving into Stage 2.

The key to balancing the alignment of your strategic goal post aligned is to focus on both internal and external perspectives – organisation priorities and shopper requirements. These two components combined provide a holistic view in ensuring that you are addressing shopper needs and developing a plan that favours your organisation.

For the majority of checkpoints created, organisations are driven to hit financial figures that look great on paper, but are imbalanced in practice. Chapter 5 details the organisational component of Stage 1, and also demonstrates the approaches to cascading your overall organisation priorities across your entire product portfolio. Chapter 6 details the shopper component of Stage 1, which involves understanding the requisite psychological positioning, pricing and marketing of your product in the market.

Once the strategic goal posts are aligned, as outlined across Chapter 5 and 6, Chapter 7 examines Stage 2's powerful pricing tactics that you can utilise to achieve the ambitions outlined in Stage 1.

Having a pricing plan in place is only part of the battle. As per my observations, circa 80% of the pricing strategy does not achieve its true potential due to poor or misaligned in-store execution.

Chapter 8 outlines guidelines for insuring your implementation is aligned to your pricing strategy and plan. The topic of execution is so vast that it is beyond the scope of this book. However, I have touched on some of the key principles in chapter 8.

SPE™ is a balanced and an end-to-end approach to pricing, and I intend to highlight key principles of the approach in this book. It connects the external shopper's decisions framework to internal organisational requirements, while ensuring that it is anchored within the market realities. The framework is designed to be embedded within the organisation to forge strong linkages between various functions.

Chapter 5
Organisational Goals

"Strategy without tactics is the slowest route to victory.
Tactics without strategy is the noise before defeat."
- Sun Tzu, Art of War

Pricing starts with your Organisational strategies and priorities

Understanding your organisation and its strategic priorities is key in establishing your pricing strategies. This is the first part of Stage 1 of the SPE™ framework. You want to ensure that your pricing strategies are in sync with the overall direction and priorities of the organisation. Does your pricing strategy influence your organisation's strategies or vice versa? Pricing should undoubtedly be dictated by your organisational strategies, but how strictly do businesses adhere to this directive when formulating their product's pricing decision?

As outlined in Chapter 3 pricing decisions are mostly made by either ensuring that you are making a 'fair' profit margin, and matching or undercutting your competitors. In most cases, the 'fair' margin is usually classified as the average margin of that class of product. Every customer, product segment and product should be able to link back to your organisation's goals. For example, an organisation selling soft drinks, the role and purpose of products as cans versus bottles, large packs versus small packs, those targeted for home consumption versus out of home consumption should be clear and linked back to your organisation's objectives. This is not just relevant for getting your price right, but influences other growth factors as well. If you are a manufacturer, your team members should be able to understand and articulate the role of a particular product within a particular customer. If you are a retailer, your team members should understand the role of a particular product in a particular category. This is the level of alignment required across your portfolio as outlined in figure 5.1.

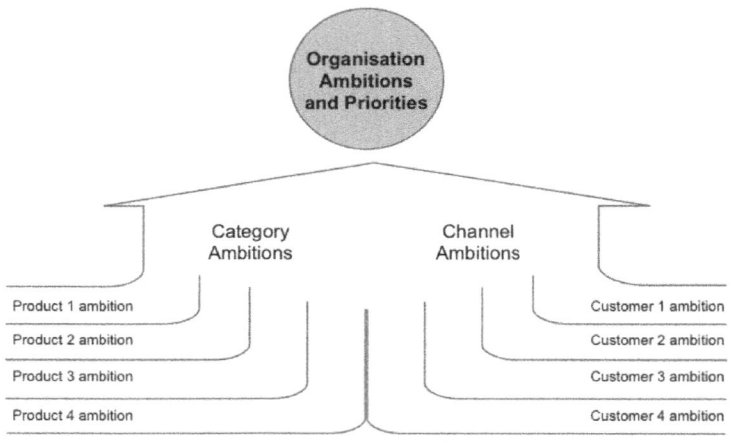

Figure 5.1: Strategic alignment across the organisation

Organisational strategies can take many forms. One should be able to filter these strategies in terms of relevance in establishing your pricing. Below are some examples:

- What are your organisation's growth ambitions across the next 3-5 years (in terms of volume and/or financial metrics)? What is more important – achieving volume or financial targets?

- Are there any product ranges and/or channels that the organisation wants to prioritise?
- Are there any major upcoming innovations in the pipeline?
- Does the organisation aspire for its products and brand to be at a premium to its competitors?
- Are there any other strategic initiatives / projects planned that are relevant to setting your price, and why?

These should give us a broad view of the overall priorities and direction of the organisation. Sometime organizations do not have these criteria documented nor understood across the teams. In such cases, you need to uncover these priorities by asking the right questions to the key decision-making stakeholders across the organisation. Keep the list of organisational priorities concise – generally 3 to 5 items is a good place to start.

REALLY understand your Organisation first

"You don't build a business - you build people – and then People build the business"
- Zig Ziglar

Understanding what's really happening in your organisation can do wonders. The best way to do so is by talking to the various key stakeholders from different departments, from juniors to seniors across the organisation. Just ask them a few simple questions like:

- What are the organisation's strengths and how should we leverage them?
- What kind of problems does their department and the organisation have and if they were the CEOs, what would they do about it?

Do this across the team (potentially 5-15 people dependant on your specific circumstances and requirements), consolidate their responses and there you have a true reflection in front of you on what is happening across the organisation and more importantly how people are feeling and working together. This is the foundation to your SWOT analysis of the organisation, and helps provide further context to your over-arching organisational priorities.

Alternatively, you can gather these insights in a workshop-based forum. If you decide to conduct a workshop for this, I would still recommend gathering some of these insights on a one-to-one basis as well. Dependant on an organisation's culture, individuals may not open up as easily in a group, while in a workshop environment the discussion is likely to be influenced by the thoughts of the senior most participant in the room. There is one critical ingredient required for gathering quality feedback – that participants are be made to feel completely comfortable in openly sharing their opinions. The bureaucratic nature of an organisation will hinder the success of this exercise. With the buy-in of and support from a senior stakeholder, one can achieve this with more ease.

Portfolio Segmentation and Assessment

Once we have had a good context of the organisation priorities, identified its true strengths and weaknesses, I recommend gaining a good understanding of your portfolio of products (and also customers in the case of a manufacturer). Ensure this level of understanding is aligned across the core members of the organisation from various departments.

The BCG Matrix is a simple, widely adopted model to segment and analyse your portfolio across 2 parameters – relative market share and market growth:

Get the Price Right

- Market share – does the product being sold have a low or high volume and or value market share?
- Market growth – are the numbers of potential shoppers or the amount they are spending in the market growing or not?

The basic idea behind it is that, the bigger the market share a product has or the faster the product's market grows, the better it is for the company. However, the version of BCG Matrix I would recommend is that of Barkdale and Harris – known as the Extended BCG Matrix, which further distinguishes the product segmentation of low market growth into low growth and declining growth market. This provides further classification on the poor performing portfolio and hence triggers the actions required in making it right.

As shown below, the 6 categories of BCG matrix are Cash cows, Stars, Dogs, Question Marks, Warhorse and Dodo.

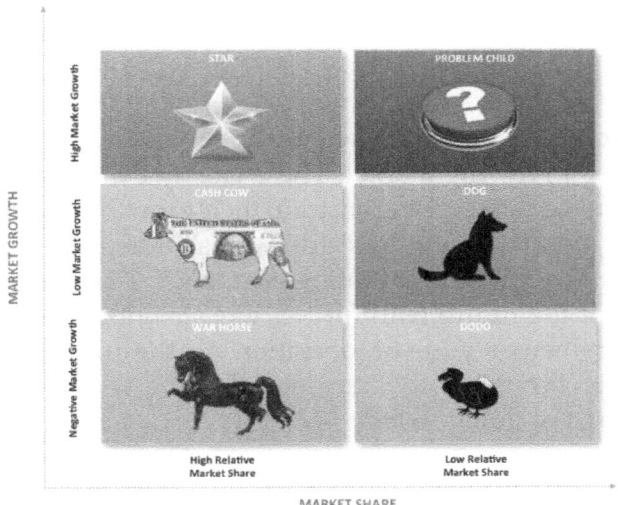

Figure 5.2: Extended BCG Matrix

Cash Cows have a high share of a slowly growing market and generate a large positive cash flow for the business. Consider what you would like to do with these members of the portfolio going forward. Would you like to harvest as much cash as possible in the short run before the 'juice' runs out of the product's life cycle? Would you like to increase your investment to defend your dominant market share or move your investment to other growing segments of the portfolio? Cash cows are sometimes the bread and butter of the organisation, and ignoring them can have significant consequences.

Stars, as the name suggests, are the top performers of your portfolio and leaders in the market. A high share of a growing market potentially makes you a market leader in that specific portfolio range. Stars are likely to be the engine for growth in many organisations. Consider again what you would like to do with these portfolio segments going forward. Would you like to further invest in them to accelerate their growth rate and keep competition at bay, or maintain the investment levels to just ride the market growth?

Question marks, also known as the Problem Child, have a low share of a growing market. These clearly exhibit immense potential, but certain factors constrain their growth. Discuss and investigate the reasons for this – do we have the right product or is there a flaw in our marketing campaign? Explore growth prospects for the future with further investments. Ask the key stakeholders across your organisation on the importance of pushing this through to the Star segment, and what would an estimated cost of doing so be?

Dogs are unattractive with very low market share in a slowly growing market. This is the tricky component of the portfolio, and discussion on it can get politicized and emotional.

Refer back to the true intention and purpose of the product, and genuinely ask what can be done about it. Do you want to continue fuelling investment in such a low return ROI profile, or liquidate the range and move your focus to other portfolio segments with more priority?

Warhorses are part of the portfolio where we have a strong market share, hence a strong cash generator, but are now part of a declining market. When a market begins to exhibit negative growth, cash cows become warhorses. What would you like to do for your warhorse portfolio? Do you want to keep persevering, until the momentum runs out or do you have the commitment and resources to influence the overall market back into growth? This might require reduced marketing expenditure or demand selective withdrawal from market segments or elimination of certain models. Please note that you just do not have to relinquish the product, but start contemplating on its subsequent version to better meet the market needs.

Dodos are part of the portfolio with low shares of a declining market. They have limited growth opportunity, and should be given serious consideration of removal from your portfolio to divert your resources to better performing segments. The timing of your market exit is critical; dependent on the level of change happening in the market space or your competitor's actions in general.

The portfolio segmentation can be constructed in 2 possible ways –in the way your internal teams are structured within the organisation or, in the way the market segments its products across the category. Sometimes both of these have the same product segmentation and sometimes they are different. You need to choose the most relevant design for your organisation.

The BCG matrix allows you to create a snapshot of your current portfolio. Try to overlay any upcoming innovations onto the matrix for reference – obviously with the guesstimates you have at your disposal. The BCG matrix is providing you with the context of your portfolio and its direction, and nothing more. Do not rely exclusively on the BCG matrix to make strategic decisions for your organisation (refer below the section on Growth Stance for further details).

In certain scenarios, market share and/or market growth could be an inadequate measure for the potential success of certain portfolios. It may not take account any other internal or external environment factors, and should be used with care.

Establish your Growth stance

You are probably wondering why we have explored the broader landscape of an organisation and its portfolio in such detail without any reference to price thus far. If pricing decisions were to be made on identifying products with a low elasticity factor (i.e. shoppers less sensitive to price) and leveraging such insights to optimise price, which would be an easy but not an optimal option in the long run. It might not even be aligned with your organisation priorities. Blindly match your price to that of a competitor's, is an easy solution, but then you would be following your competitor's strategy instead of your own.

Now we come to the crux of a really important question. What are your aspirations for your portfolio of products and customers?

I found my answer from Simon Launay, CEO and founder of arlians. Simon developed the concept of assigning a growth stance across the portfolio, which acts as a bridge between your organisation's priorities and your portfolio.

"The principle of a good strategy is connecting the "as is" to the "to be". Without it organisations often fail to reconcile what THEY WANT with what THEY CAN with what THEY OUGHT to do. The Grow Maintain Restage (GMR) is critical to anchoring a sense of reality around what will it take to achieve the goals, can they be achieved if at all and critically, at what cost to the business."
- Simon Launay

Growth stance can be of 3 types – Grow, Maintain and Restage:

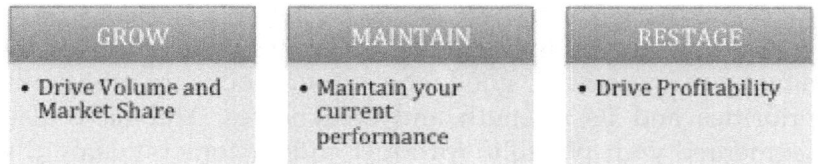

Figure 5.3: Three categories of growth stance

1. **Grow** – Do you want to grow your market share? Volume is more important as a KPI in comparison to profit, and the focus is on volume driving initiatives. E.g. increase promotional spending or pushing harder on larger pack range across the portfolio etc. The volume growth does not necessarily have to come at the expense of profit. There are ways to manage both.

2. **Maintain** – Do you want to simply maintain the market share and/or profit levels within a certain range for your portfolio? If you choose to maintain both the market share and profit, you need to state which of these has a slightly higher priority. For products and customers at the Maintain stage, we do not need to increase or decrease our level of focus, but to do enough to maintain their performance. In some cases, your Cash Cow portfolio range could demand

a lot of investment to just maintain their position at current levels.

3. **Restage** – Do you want to increase your profit margin? Profit is more important as a KPI compared to volume here. This could be to recover profit on products with relatively low profit margins (e.g. Stars) or increasing profit on the Cash Cow range of products to boost the overall profitability of the organisation. The profit growth does not necessarily have to come at the expense of volume. There are ways to attain both.

So, how do you to assign G-M-R across your portfolio? By now, you possess a good context of your organisation's priorities and its strength and weaknesses. You have also segmented your portfolio (product and customers) using the BCG matrix. Leveraging these insights while simultaneously using 3 additional analytical charts will equip you to designate your growth stance. These 3 charts are outlined below:

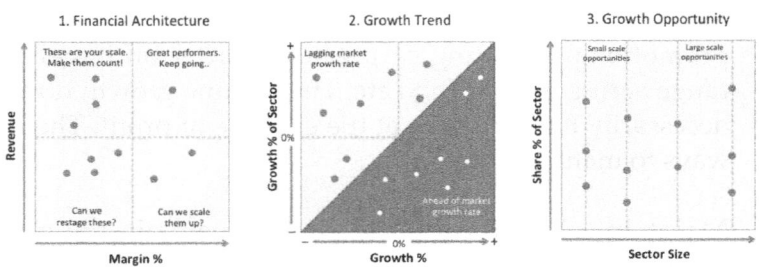

Figure 5.4: Growth stance charts

Get the Price Right

Chart 1 – Financial Architecture

This chart segments your portfolio across two internally driven dimensions – revenue and profit margins. If you prefer, you can replace revenue with a volume KPI as well. Although at first this appears to be very similar to the BCG matrix, it is not.

The chart analyses the importance of each product/product groups to the overall business performance in terms of both SCALE and PROFITABILITY. Can you identify the range that drives 80% of your SCALE? Which products are profit boosting and which ones are profit draining?

Chart 2 – Growth Trend

The chart helps to identify your position relative to your competitors' across the portfolio. The two dimensions are organisational growth % versus market growth %. The chart acts as a good benchmark of our performance in the market. If one of our products were growing at 10%, would you classify it to be good performer? Well, it depends on the relative growth rate of the market. If the market is growing at 30%, then your 10% growth rate is hardly making a positive mark.

The chart can help identify growth opportunities (where organisational growth lags behind market growth) and also identify potential competitive threats (where organisational growth is ahead of the market growth).

Chart 3 – Market Scale

This chart is effective in depicting the scale of the market itself across different product ranges, and how significant the size of the organisation is in each of them. The two dimensions of the chart are organisation size versus market size, and can be measured in terms of either revenue or volume. The chart helps us to examine if a certain identified opportunity is worth pursuing.

To further improve the insights from these charts, you can overlay data of multiple time periods on the same chart. For example, Chart 1 can have two bubbles for each product / product group – one for the year 2015 and the other for 2013. In such an instance, the chart would demonstrate how your portfolio has evolved across the 3-year period.

The potential of these charts is realized when they are used simultaneously to assign the growth stance across your portfolio. I strongly recommend doing this exercise as a joint cross-functional team to gain maximum insights from the participants and engage in debate-led outcome. On a few occasions, you will struggle to assign the growth stance – simply make a note that this is the case, and make your best possible decision between Grow-Maintain-Restage.

The above growth stances should be assigned across your entire portfolio, starting from the top of the hierarchy range to the bottom. This can be applied at total product level and total customer / channel levels, and then expanded to include the matrix in between. You can find the growth stance template on www.GetThePriceRightBook.com.

As explained earlier, the portfolio can potentially be constructed in 2 ways –in the way your internal teams are structured within the organisation and in the way the market segments its product portfolio across the category. As mentioned earlier, choose the one most suited to your case.

Leverage Product Life cycle

You should consider the stage of your product's life cycle in determining your growth stance. The chart below depicts the 4 stages of a product overlaid with the segments of the extended BCG matrix by Barksdale & Harris. There is an additional category referenced here – infants.

Infants are new products, which generally have a high degree of risk. They may not immediately earn profits and consume substantial cash resources.

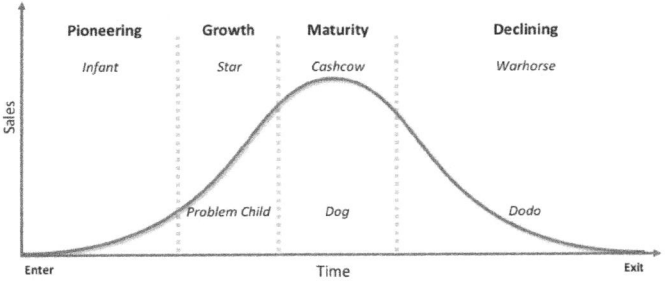

Figure 5.5: Product life cycle
(simplified for demonstration purpose only)

Products in the Pioneering and Growth phases are likely to be assigned a growth stance, unless profitability is of significant concern. This is where products are required to be pushed in the market to drive SCALE.

For the Declining phase, given its stage in the product life cycle, it is likely to be assigned a restage stance to maximise returns before the next version of the product is launched as infants in the Pioneering stage.

In regards to the Maturity stage, there might not be any preference to its growth stance. The preference outlined here for a growth stance is just a suggestion. It is possible that you would like to ensure that your Star range is generating a good level of profits, or that the warehouse is generating enough volume to keep the race on for little longer compared to your competitors.

Every scenario is to be assessed on its own merit.

Modeling your Growth Stance

Once you have completed your growth stance matrix, re-assess it to ensure it is aligned with your overall organisational priorities, and its strengths and weaknesses are taken into consideration in making your decisions as joint cross-functional teams. This will significantly help you in the future in ensuring that you are consistent across the board, from your strategy to pricing and eventually its execution.

Every customer, every product segment, every product can now be linked back to your organisational priorities. If you have effectively achieved this, the chances are bright that you are already ahead in your thinking in comparison to your competition. Bravo!

To effectively undertake this exercise, systematic financial modelling should support the above analysis. One can effectively stress test the likely success rate of your GMR stances by evaluating the impact of your decisions on both internal financials and external market shares.

When we deployed these analytics to support the strategic stance of our clients, we were able to adapt our approach to better suit the risk profile of the organisation. I strongly recommend you include analytics as part of your analysis.

Get the Price Right

Growth stance is only half of the work done for setting your strategic goal post of the SPE™ framework. The other half is the shopper lens, which will be covered in the next chapter.

Chapter 6
Shopper Goals is Your Key to Positioning

"Your customer doesn't care how much you know until they know how much you care."
- Damon Richards

Identify your battleground and positioning tactics

Now we come to the second but equally important part of the strategic element of the SPE™ framework.

To ensure our value equation is optimised for the shoppers, we need to support the growth stances (as discussed in Chapter 5) with a clear understanding of our desired product positioning with our shoppers within the marketplace. This begs the question of what the shopper needs and how we should position our product portfolio accordingly.

Shoppers have various needs, but this does not mean the organisation should cater for every one of them. The topic of whether a product should find a niche in the marketplace or be offered at an irresistible price to the shopper is a vast one and can be found in any major marketing book, articles, journals, etc. For the premises of Getting the Price Right, we will touch base on a few key fundamentals of product features and positioning. After all, developing the pricing strategy and tactics should be systematically linked to your product portfolio strategy as well.

The objective is that, wherever we may choose to play in the market, we should be clear in our positioning and the competitor set. Each different set of competitors has their own price spectrum. Choosing your competitor set can influence your price point, potential sales volume, margins and the way you market your products in the marketplace.

There are 3 stages in defining your desired positioning with your shoppers:

1. Identify your shopper's requirements
2. Identify your competitor base
3. Align on your target shopper group and price positioning

To ensure our value equation is superior to that of a competitor's product, we will delve deeper into understanding both sides of the scale – the scale of perceived value and the scale of pain.

The perceived value will be a key tool in understanding the required psychological positioning, pricing and marketing of your product on the shelves.

Identify what your shopper wants

Missions, benefits and features

Each time a shopper picks up a product from the shelf, therein lays a purpose. The purpose can appear to be very explicit or ambiguous at times, but this does not change the fact that there is always a purpose behind the shopper purchasing a product. These purposes can also be referred to as shopper missions. In another words, the shopper is on a mission to fulfil a desired goal. To fulfil its desired goal, the shopper buys a product with the desired benefits. A benefit answers the basic question, "So What?" Product benefits are delivered via a set of product features.

It is important to distinguish between these 3 terminologies. Mission is a purpose for the shopper to buy in the first place, features tell you what the product is, and benefits are what sell it. For example, a shopper is hungry and therefore is on a mission to satisfy his hunger. In order to do so, the shopper may be on a hunt for a product with high sugar content (feature) to boost energy (benefit), spicy flavours (feature) to satisfy his taste buds (benefit) and a branded product (feature) to avoid any disappointments (perceived benefit).

So our task here is to identify:

a) shopper missions,
b) desired product benefits as perceived by the shopper, and
c) key features of the products.

Shopper research and analysis

These specific shopper missions and product benefits can be identified by directly consulting a targeted shopper base via surveys or by analysing a large shopper panel database. The best outputs are when you combine both of these methods together – a good balance between both qualitative and quantitative research results. For tips on structuring an effective survey, visit www.Getthepricerightbook.com.

It is critical that the core team for the product development is highly involved in this process. The question to the shoppers is a simple one – what triggered their purchase in the first place? You are likely to get some varied responses, but after the first few responses, and with a bit of creativity, you can start to consolidate them into a few key themes.

Let us take a simplified example of a chocolate bar. We can start by asking the relevant set of sampled shoppers why they buy chocolates in general (i.e. the shopper missions). How do they think a chocolate bar could help them? How many times would they buy in a month and on average how much would they spend per trip? A simplified example is shown in Table 6.1 for two shopper missions – 'Hunger Treat' and 'Sharing with a buddy'.

A more detailed example can be found on www.GetThePriceRightBook.com

No.	Shopper Mission	Description of Shopper Missions	Key Associated Product Benefits	Average number of trips per month	Average spend per trip (£)	Total spend (value size) per month
1	Hunger Treat	Having a chocolate when I am hungry or need energy booster from sugar	Quick release of energy Tasty treat for my taste buds Easy to eat on the go	3	£1.50	£4.50
2	Self Indulging	Treating myself with a chocolate as a token of self-reward	Dark chocolate, and less sweet Branded product to treat myself	1	£2	£4
... and so on. Other shopper missions can be Sharing occasion, Gifting occasion and more...						

Table 6.1: Shopper segmentation
(simplified for demonstration purposes)

I would not propose, at this stage, to ask shoppers what product features are most attractive to them. Humans usually do not naturally think of features when purchasing and consuming the products.

A product feature or a set of features automatically gets translated into perceived benefits in most cases, and that is what they usually recall at a later stage. A strong brand presence of a product will also influence the shopper in remembering a specific product instead of the product benefit. For example, when asked about what chocolate they would prefer when they are hungry, the response could be either a) a product that satisfies my hunger and taste buds, and/or b) a specific preferred product such as Snickers. The shopper would rarely mention a chocolate bar that has a 10% sugar level or something that is covered with a highly reflective aluminium cover.

This explains why there is emphasis on focusing on the actual value to the shopper instead of extolling the great features of your product.

Identify your potential competitor base

A recent global retail shopper study by marketing giant Ogilvy & Mather entitled "Shopper Decisions Made In-Store" revealed that 38% to 88% of shoppers make their decision in-store regarding which category to buy from, which brand to choose and how much they will buy. It means that, even if the shoppers are clear regarding their mission, there is a strong chance that they have not decided on a specific brand or product in advance. The competition is active both inside and outside of the store, and you require a good level of understanding of who your competitors are.

You can identify your competitors by conducting shopper surveys and shopper behaviour analysis, visiting stores to view product merchandising and questioning key stakeholders within your organisation.

If you are a manufacturer, you could also ask your customers (the retailers) as they are responsible for setting the store fixtures and deciding on product ranges in the store. Shopper behaviors are very much shaped by the store format and style, and hence retailers put a significant level of energy and resources into ensuring that they are fit for purpose. Products that are placed next to each other on the shelves are generally going to have stronger direct competition.

Observing how the relevant category aisle is arranged in a store can illustrate a visual landscape of the market. As a rule of thumb, the size and space a product occupies on the shelf is a good indicator of its overall market share. Competing products are usually kept in close proximity to one another to give shoppers a better and easier choice to fulfill their shopper missions.

For each shopper mission, you need to identify your potential competitor set, and their product features as perceived by the shoppers. Similar to step 1, this information can be obtained via shopper surveys or by evaluating a large shopper panel database.

When evaluating which competitor set to consider, encourage yourself to think beyond the core category of your product. In the case of satisfying your hunger, chocolates could potentially take many forms, such as standard chocolate blocks, thin and long bars, flavoured chocolate with nuts or something that has more wafers in it. Each type of chocolate could cater to a different spectrum of price bracket that you could demand from the shoppers. We haven't factored in the effect of branding, as more premium products (as perceived by the shoppers) could charge a premium price.

Ask shoppers to identify and rate the key features that they find relevant to their shopper mission. These ratings can provide a good overview of the product from a shopper's perspective. Leverage shopper data to get insight of market share, average price and average price per unit (in grams or milliliters).

A sample data set, including demonstration of a list and rating of product features, can be found on www.GetThePriceRightBook.com.

Competing with a competitor at a higher price bracket could mean that you are likely to set your price within that price bracket. However, it does not mean that you could charge a price exactly the same as your competitors. For this to happen, the perceived net value to the shopper should be at par with that of your competitors. We will cover this in more depth in Chapter 7.

A lot of this information might already be part of the product development process or the marketing campaigns, and can therefore be leveraged quite easily. However, there are instances where the organisation's intended competitors and the shoppers perceived competitors were different. Receiving the true voice of shoppers can be very insightful for this purpose.

Align on your target shopper group and price positioning

If product costs establish a lower limit, below which prices are not viable in the long term, then the upper limit of your pricing is a combination of affordability of your target shoppers, how they perceive the value of your product, and how it compares to your competitor's product range. Your pricing level is determined based on where you play (in this case these are the shopper missions) and whom you play with (your competitors).

Step 1 articulated the landscape of the shopper missions and the benefits shoppers are seeking for it. Step 2 outlined the key competitor set within each shopper mission. Now all you need to align are your priority shopper mission(s) and your key competitor sets.

For existing products, you already have an established competitor base, and would require a significant level of alterations in your marketing plans to make any changes. For new products, you have more flexibility in making such decisions at this early stage. The decision of which shopper mission to go after is dominantly driven by the overall organisation, product portfolio strategy and market growth dynamics. Several options can be developed and evaluated with a good mix of cross-functional team engagement and structured financial modelling. For a self-indulging shopper mission, do you want to compete with a standard or a premium chocolate bar range? Would you sell it in a form of a standard one-time-eat bar size or have more bite-size shaped chocolates in a bag for munching purposes as well? As long as our product features deliver the right set of benefits for the shopper in addressing their shopper missions, it is good to go.

We do not necessarily need to win against our competitors every time or play to fight for every shopper mission. Your organisational strategy from Chapter 5 should also help you with this analysis. Try to leverage the organisational strategy, organisational stance, and portfolio strategy to further help you decide on your product positioning. For instance, if a product is assigned a growth stance to GROW, where the intention is to grow volume and market share ahead of profitability, align your positions with the right competitors that drive SCALE. On the other hand, if your growth stance is RESTAGE, align your competitor set that could help with delivering lower cost per kg or higher price per kg, and hence higher profitability.

Be cautious of choosing the right shopper missions and competitor set for your products. A car dealer wanting to increase the profitability of his business could consider transitioning from selling Toyota cars to the more luxurious Aston Martin. This would help the dealership increase its profitability per car, but will also have a huge impact on the sell volume, and a possibility of reduction in the overall profitability level.

In regard to more moderate situations, at this stage there would seem to be some compromise being considered between gaining market scale and increasing profitability, but that can be balanced with some of the powerful techniques outlined in Chapter 7. For now, just ensure that the organisation is aligned with the competitor set within each of the shopper missions that you would like to pursue.

Chapter 7
Pricing Excellence in Action

"Retail is the theater for a brand so write the script, set the stage, and take the customer to another place."
- David Ogilvy

Chapter 5 and Chapter 6 have laid a strong foundation with a coherent internal and external led ambitions and priorities of the SPE™ framework. We have a good understanding of the organisation strategies and their alignment to the pricing tactics, growth ambitions and key strengths and weaknesses across the portfolio, key shopper missions and understanding as to why shoppers are buying in the first place, key competitor sets for us to measure against and the benefits / features that the shoppers are looking for in the products.

This chapter is where we write the pricing theatre script and prepare to go on the Retail stage. We will take our analysis further by diving into the practical applications of pricing excellence - the second stage of the SPE™ framework. There are several sections within this chapter. You can either read them in sequence or jump to the topic that interests you most. However the information still refers to the information and techniques shared in previous chapters.

Price is not always logical

Is pricing logical all the time? No, pricing doesn't have to be logical; it just needs to work. When we raise our prices on a pack of crisps in a retail store, logic says customers are likely to notice the price hike and hence there will be some drop in the volume being sold. However, sometimes volume is not impacted at all. Similarly ever wonder why retailers and manufacturers still stock up and aim to sell poor performing products even at a dirt-cheap price in store? Logic would say let's rationalise the portfolio and keep only the winners on the shelves.

However, we have countless examples of the times when the actions or outcomes were completely different. We know how pricing balances the perceived value of the value equation, but it also has the power to change your perceived value of the product itself. When psychology and emotions (largely driven by System 1 of the mental process) come into play, logic (which is System 2 of the mental process) doesn't have to be right all the time.

RELATIVE COMPETITIVE PRICING

In convincing the shopper to pick up your products, the shopper's value equation should be in your favour and the mental process (System 1 or System 2 or both) should have favoured your product in comparison to that of your competitor. The question usually arises as to how your pricing should be in comparison to your competitors. Should we go through the route of differentiation or cost price or market niche strategy? These are Porter's generic strategies, and can be too simplistic for an organisation to embed.

Bowman's Strategy Clock

In 1996, Cliff Bowman and David Faulkner developed Bowman's Strategy Clock. This model of corporate strategy extends Porter's three strategic positions to eight, and presents

Get the Price Right

options for competitive positioning according to price level (cost advantage strategy) or the level of perceived added value (a differentiation advantage strategy), as demonstrated in figure 7.1. The model also identifies the likelihood of success for each strategy. Clock positions from 4 to 6 are certainly doomed to fail, so understand if the organisation is heading towards this direction well in advance. Positions 1 to 3 potentially support differentiation and niche strategy. Positions 7 and 8 support low-cost strategy.

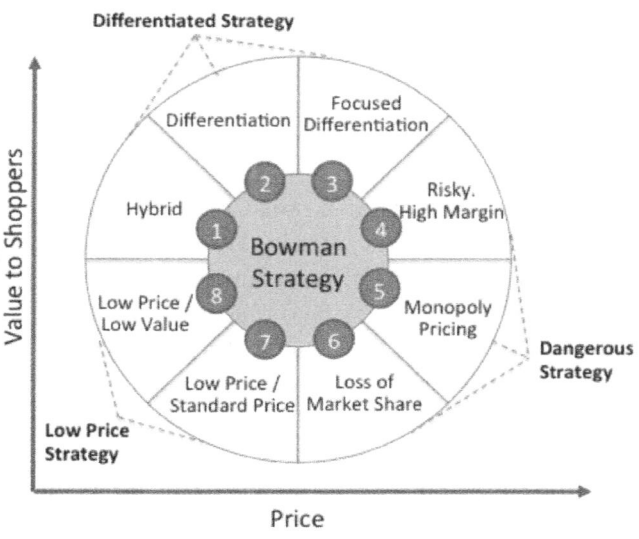

Figure 7.1: Bowman's Strategy Clock

I would recommend that you assign both your current (actual) pricing and the pricing that you aspire to have on the clock. Do this for both your, and your competitor's, product range. Are any of your products or that of your competitors placed in the 4 to 6 range? Review your feedback from the shoppers (as per Chapter 6) to gauge your position on the clock. Were there any shopper missions where your products were inferior in the eyes of the shoppers compared to those provided by competitors, and you are still charging a similar rate?

When your entire portfolio is placed on the clock, it can either be concentrated on certain segments or spread across the clock. For example, Godiva chocolate is a luxury brand, and the majority of its products would be placed within the differentiated and niche strategy segments. On the other hand, Cadbury chocolates are ranged from everyday standard Dairy Milk chocolates to more premium range in boxes for gifting. A more diverse pricing portfolio is acceptable as long as it doesn't contradict its brand positioning in the marketplace.

Promo versus non-promo positioning

A product can have multiple positioning on the clock based on its pricing structure. Let us take an example of a chocolate bar - a category with very high volume sold on deal (VSOD). The same product can occupy two places on the clock – when it is on and off promotion. Chocolate bars at a promoted price could have been placed around section 7 – 8 on the clock, with strong value for money and potentially positive value equation. Products are inferior but the prices are attractive enough to convince consumers to try them once. The opposite could be true when the product is off promotions, with potentially being placed on the danger zone of the clock.

You can find further examples how different types of promotions can be used to support your pricing strategies on www.GetThePriceRightBook.com.

Financial Modelling and Assessment

The above analysis should be supported with both qualitative and quantitative inputs. The results on the clock

Get the Price Right

board should also be supported with analytical modelling of the market and by accessing how your sales are impacted at different price points. How price sensitive are shoppers to your products versus that of your competitors? Is there a trigger level, beyond which price either increases or decreases significantly? Modelling exercise can help assess the impact of variation in prices on both internal financial metrics and external market share. For example, if the clock is suggesting that you should lower your price to move from the position 5 (current) to 7 (our aspiration), but the financials (our feasibility test) does not support the move – we are in a deadlock.

Other growth levers to consider

What this means is that other factors, beyond pricing alone, need to be considered to increase the survivability and growth of the product. This forces the organisation to explore other growth levers within the organisation. Can the organisation reduce costs to sustain lower prices, or push its marketing campaign to enhance its brand image and therefore the perceived value of the product? Can the product be further enhanced to ensure it better addresses shopper requirements and competes well within the marketplace? Price is one of the strongest levers for growth, but on occasions, it has its limits as well. By being proactive on realising the limitation of price and acting accordingly at the back of it will help the organisation tweak its plan in time before it's too late.

Chapter 6 helped us understand our pricing barometer by identifying your competitor set. This exercise can help your gauge an overall pricing strategy and specific levels in comparison to your competitor set.

Sahaj Kothari

PRICE ANCHORING AND 3T™ FRAMEWORK

Is there ever a time that one Budweiser beer is worth more than another? Logic would dictate that this answer be "no," but bar hoppers know that just isn't the case. Where you buy is just as important as what you buy. In a Vanderbilt University study published in the New York Times Magazine, customers were willing to pay higher prices for a Budweiser if they knew it was coming from an upscale hotel versus a run-down grocery store. The context can have a huge impact on your perceived value of the product. The perceived prestige of the upscale hotel allowed it to get away with charging higher prices.

Would you pay $10 for a standard bottle of beer? Is that very expensive or cheap? Again, different shoppers would respond to it differently, and are influenced by their own experiences and the associations in their mind. When given the opportunity for the shopper to buy $10 beer, the shopper's mental process taps into his or her own relevant associations using System 1. If those associations justify spending $10, you are likely to sell the bottle of beer, but the reverse is also true. Place a $10 bottle next to a $50 bottle; research has shown that you will definitely sell more of the $10 bottles. Why the difference? Now the shoppers are associating $10 with both their experiences and what they observe in the store, and will respond to the one that has stronger emotions attached to it. $10 might be just a bit expensive for the shopper, but all of a sudden the $50 option makes it 5 times cheaper. The word 'cheaper' is subconsciously resonating in the shopper's mental process, and the purchase is made. This technique is so powerful that, even if the shopper knows how the prices have been structured in such a way, it still works.

Get the Price Right

Multi level pricing to help anchor your price

Is the glass half full or half empty? Well, it surely depends on your context and the relevant anchor frame, doesn't it?

Could you be leaving profits on the table just because you aren't offering enough pricing options? Several major organisations use this technique to increase their sales on their leading range or the ones with the growth stance as GROW. According to William Poundstone, author of the book Priceless: The Myth of Fair Value, it's very likely that this is the case. In his book, Poundstone examines the purchasing patterns of consumers on a selection of beer. In the first test, there were only two options available: a regular option and a premium option.

Test 1:

$1.80 $2.50
20%   80%

The verdict was clear, and 80% of the people choose the more premium option. $2.50 was the winner in this case. However could adding a third item and price point increase revenue? The researchers tested this by adding a $1.60 beer to the menu to see if people would prefer to pay less on their beer.

Test 2:

This time anchoring to a cheaper beer worked adversely to our performance. The cheap beer was ignored and it reversed the ratio of standard to premium purchases. This was clearly the wrong choice, since in this instance anchoring is actually playing a negative role. If customers don't want a cheaper beer, perhaps a more expensive beer might work?

Test 3:

Perfect! We found our sweet spot for now. By having an even higher premium product, more shoppers bought $2.50 beer option. These examples clearly show how important it is to test out different brackets of pricing. You can find further examples of promotion tactics on www.GetThePriceRightBook.com.

Get the Price Right

3T™ framework – Trade in, Trade up & Trade across

Multi-level pricing gives more options to the shoppers, and thus allows us to expand our reach to the shoppers. What else does the experiment helps us understand? There are other powerful physiological behaviours of the shoppers, which I refer to as 3T™ framework - Trade In, Trade Up and Trade Across.

In most cases, shoppers tend to go for the middle option – so make sure you are positioning your desired WINNING sku in the middle where possible. This is where most of your shoppers are likely to purchase. The left most option is equally important in attracting or trading in shoppers on the lower price spectrum that would not have bought any beers if such an option were not available. 5% of purchases on the $1.80 option could have been the lost opportunity if this bottle size / price point was not available. In most cases, especially for new products, a lower price point product allows shoppers to test the product before they start spending more for it. Having a strong lower price point product could be the strong penetrative driver for the organisation. Imagine if in the above example these beer options were from a newly established brand. I would then expect more shoppers to buy the $1.80 option regardless of how many premium options were available in the marketplace. In fact, if you would like to drive penetration, you could discount the $1.80 price point to $1. More shoppers are likely to get enticed with the offer and give it a try.

In a similar way, in the above example, we were able to upgrade certain shoppers from $2.50 to $3.40 price option, which we would have lost if only £1.80 and $2.50 price options were available. Some customers are always going to want the most expensive option, so adding a super-premium price will give them that option and will make your other prices look better by comparison. In fact we could try raising the $3.40 to $5 and evaluate the net impact. The right most option should be the premium option with certain features that are unique to it. You can always find someone who is willing to pay more, but not having the option to make the sale is a lost opportunity. In some cases, it is possible that the most premium option attracts a completely new set of shoppers (those who wouldn't have bought any of the beer in Test 2). The most premium option could either be the most profitable option (highest price per unit) for the organisation or the one delivering the strongest value (cost per unit) to the shoppers. Either of them could be classified as the premium TRADE UP pack.

Once you have TRADED IN a strong base of shoppers to your brand, refocus your promotional campaign on more of the premium products to TRADE them UP. This allows keeping your shoppers within your portfolio, while diversifying your portfolio for a stronger sustainability base. Once you have a good level of shopper base, you can position your portfolio to TRADE ACROSS between different product categories. For example, shoppers could be offered the above range of beers alongside some peanut snacks for a sell across opportunity. Once the shoppers buy beer, some of them could consider buying snacks to compliment their beer consumption experience. There you go, now you have the ability to not optimise your beer category, but leveraging beer to sell your snack category as well.

Sandwich pricing

Another powerful application of using 3T™ framework, an anchored leveraged multi-level pricing, is to 'sandwich' the offers of your competitors to maximum shopper switching from their products to yours. In the above example, if the $2.50 price option happened to be from one of our major competitors, we could introduce two products $1.70 and $3.40 – one tapping into the lower price seeking shoppers and the other catering for a more premium experience. This would result in 'squeezing' your competitor's $1.80 price product from either side.

Conclusion

Having a multi-level price options gives the shoppers the flexibility to purchase the product as suited to their requirements. Reflecting back to Chapter 6 on shopper missions, requirements and positioning, having a multi-level pricing range allows the organisation to expand the number of shoppers they can target and hence optimise the overall revenue opportunities. Your product positioning is key in establishing your price bands in the first place. Of course your product should also give the experience of the price band the shoppers are paying for, or else you won't have enough repeat purchases. The first impression of your product positioning can sway the buyer from not buying to buying your product from the shelves. Even in tough market conditions, you have the opportunity to GROW or RESTAGE as per your desire.

PRICE INCREASES EVEN IN TOUGH CONDITIONS

It's been too long since you last had any price increases. The high rate of inflation has been adversely hitting your bottom line performance. You are worried that, if this continues, losses won't be sustainable. At the same time any price increases can be a sensitive topic with how shoppers might react. If you are a manufacturer, you know facing the retailer for another price increase push in such a challenging market is not going to land well.

Yes, everyone understands that inflation is all around us, but still it's not an easy pill to digest. We hope that competitors might be in a similar situation, but still afraid to take the first step in the marketplace. With a product with a growth stance of RESTAGE, profitability is one of your key concerns, but in most cases that can't come without a disastrous impact on the volume you sell. Your ambition is to increase your profitability rate and the total level of profits at the same time. If you go for a price increase, and your competitors do not follow you, the stakes can be high and risky.

Inflation is a number one trigger point and driver for price increases for the majority of the organisations. It is only until an organisation's profits start to get impacted that a mini project is usually initiated within the organisation to hike up the prices across all the products affected by inflation. Some organisations have a pricing policy of simply raising their prices in line with inflation or the standard national inflation rate. The latter option sometimes appears to be easier in convincing retailers (in the case of manufacturers) or shoppers (in the case of retailers) that they really don't want to have any price increases, but is a result of just challenging economic conditions.

This does not have to be the case, and of course there are better ways. For times when you are looking for a price increase in a competitive market, driven by inflation or other drivers, this section explores 4 potential methods you could incorporate in such scenarios to ensure the risks are minimised.

1. NPD ammunition
2. Diversify your price increases
3. Price memory
4. Get your pack right

This gives you a higher chance of success. You can even mix some of these principles in building your pricing strategies. I have successfully adopted these principles with my clients, and they can work for you too.

Get the Price Right

1. NPD ammunition

Given the circumstances outlined above, you could tap into your arsenal of upcoming innovative products of the organisation. This is particularly relevant for manufacturers trying to strengthen their value proposition in the marketplace and always trying to bring something new and refreshing for their shoppers. Introduction of new products within your product portfolio can also help you establish new price points in the marketplace.

If you are currently selling 100g of strawberry flavoured jelly beans at $2 a bag, could you introduce a mixed berry flavoured 100g bag of strawberry and blueberries for $2.25? $2.25 is just an example and should relate back to value equation for the shoppers and whether or not it makes sense from the internal operations and financials of doing so. The point is that an introduction of new products can be leverage to re-establish a different price point along with re-positioning your product range, if that is what you are looking for. This approach can help an organisation with both growth stances of RESTAGE and GROW across their portfolio.

There are two key benefits of such method. Firstly you are less likely to have an adverse impact on your volume compared to if you just had a price increase on the original single flavour bag at $2. In fact this method gives you an opportunity to a) increase the overall volume you sell as you are giving more shoppers more choices, and b) improve your product mix as some of your standard shoppers are now going to upgrade from spending $2 to $2.25. From a price point of view, all of a sudden shoppers expect to pay an amount other than just $2, even if the competitors are still at $2. This is also a powerful signal to competitors to re-think their pricing strategy. Of course you can't influence their decision directly, but your actions can trigger their thinking in a certain direction. You should plan to be at least one step ahead of your competitors. Such pricing techniques would work even better with the multi-level tiered pricing (refer to section 3 tier pricing for further details).

What you achieve beyond the introduction of the new product is up to your organisation's aspiration and execution excellence. If you would like to move more shoppers to a $2.25 price level in the long run, you can start pushing more of the $2.25 range on the shelves, until you feel you have enough migration of shoppers to such new products and the price sensitivity of moving away from $2 is within your tolerance level. Obviously there are practical limits to how you can execute such tactics, primarily driven by the limited shelf space. Of course migration of shoppers can take time, and if the sku rationalisation lens is applied too soon, at the early stages of the strategy, there is a chance for the retailer to either de-list less performing range (in terms of scale) or do not list the product in the first place itself. The trick is for both manufacturers and retailers to get on board on the longer-term vision and strategy, and support it with the joint execution plan.

2. Diversify your price increases

Inflation is real and it affects everyone in some shape or form. The impact of inflation could be marginal for some but detrimental to other organisations. Retail environment is particularly sensitive to inflation, and it is a hot topic for them all the time. Getting operational costs under control is one of the largest challenges for a retailer, where the business model is usually based on surviving on low margins and strong cash flow models. With so much price inflation in recent years with commodities price rising, salaries of highly skilled work force rising and so much fluctuation in oil prices, the majority of retailers' and manufacturers' costs are on the rise. Shoppers, usually those in the low and middle-income families, have less to spend under high inflation times. Their spending on shopping has increased, while their salaries have not increased at the same rate.

An alternative approach to a standard price hike across the entire portfolio should be to tactfully drive your product and brand portfolio in the way you want. You can be selective in picking up certain products that drive maximum results, i.e. price increases on selective products that drive maximum profit generating opportunity and could potentially balance out the total inflation cost across the entire portfolio. Ensure your pricing is aligned across the portfolio with your desire to recover profit (restage) or gain market share (grow).

Segment your products across price elasticity factors, i.e. shoppers less sensitive to price movements, and the switching rate (i.e. shopper brand loyalty) compared to that of your competitors. The figure 7.2 on the next page depicts the four quadrants of this matrix and recommends potential actions for you to consider.

You can even shout about your price increases to your shoppers to gain traction in a positive way. For instance, if you have applied a price increase to only 30% of your portfolio, you can indicate to shoppers that while competitors have passed on the inflation cost, you have not done so for the majority (70%) of the product range. In terms of the value equation for the shopper, such marketing does not raise the perceived value of the product, but helps reduce the pain side of the value scale. In some situations, you might not recover your entire inflation cost by raising prices on only a few products, but such marketing publicity might just be enough to grow your profit base as a whole. Inflation can be your blessing in disguise, if you use it wisely.

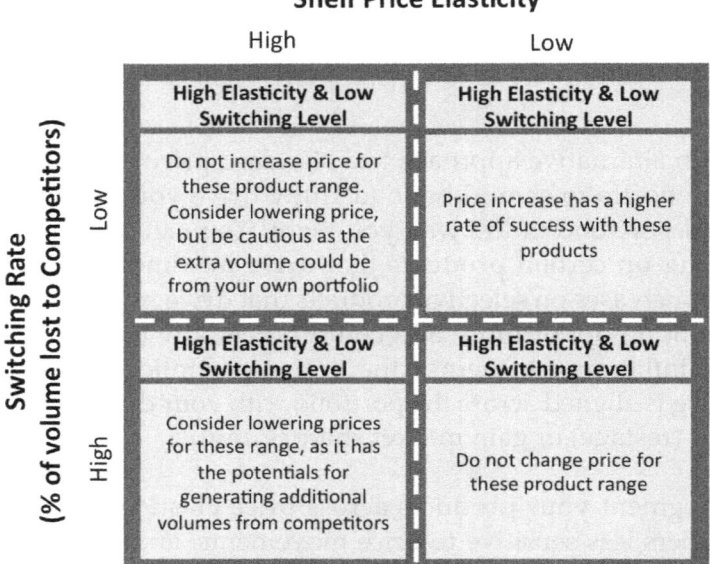

Figure 7.2: Elasticity and switching matrix

3. Price memory

Shoppers can be very sensitive to price increases in the marketplace, given the vast amount of alternative offers in the store fighting for their attention. Evaluating the value equation of a product, unless it's previously backed up by extremely strong positive shopper experiences and unbeatable brand loyalty, and getting the price right is key. The challenge is, after a while the shoppers get trained to expect a certain price for a product. A specific price for a product is anchored in their minds to a singular and simple number – which are harder to just change.

Get the Price Right

On the other hand, the perceived value of the product is somewhat subjective and can vary with your specific circumstances at the time of purchase. You are more likely to appreciate having an ice-cream on a hot day instead of a cold day; you are likely to buy that frozen pizza you wanted on your way back home after a long tiring day at work rather than on a Sunday when you might have plenty of time on hand to cook yourself. The perceived value of a product can change, but the price is relatively stuck in the minds of the shoppers. This effect is further amplified if the majority of the key products and brands within the category have anchored to one single price.

A way to re-condition the shopper perception is to keep implementing regular price increases across your portfolio. Don't wait for your inflation or external factors to trigger your thinking about it, but have a well-planned price increase program laid out across multiple years in advance. Instead of implementing large price increases every 2-3 years, you could deploy marginal price increases every year in smaller chunks. By regularly implementing price increases and with small 'pain' levels each time, shoppers do not hold onto a single price point. With regular price changes, shoppers' strength to associate a product to a specific price is greatly minimised, which gives us the flexibility to both influence and adapt to shopper behaviours with time. As counterintuitive as it may seem, following this approach can reduce both the level of risk and the complexity of executing a price increase.

An important factor to consider is the timing of such regular price increases. You can either align such price increases to your internal processes, such as the start of your annual planning cycle, or follow the market norm of your category, which usually can be January of every year. There is no right answer to it, and you would need to assess the timing based on your specific situation. Do you feel it's better to push through the prices at similar or different times than when competitors would do? This approach allows you to have a price increase on certain products in advance of when the inflation is going to hit. The trick is, of course, not to dismantle the shopper's value equation in doing so.

4. Get your pack right

Sometimes, no matter what, a price increase scenario is just a very risky option on the table. In the scenario where the category is already anchored to key established price points and competitors are showing no signs to move their prices, what do you do? You have tried every avenue to test pricing options for growth, but all are suggesting one thing – do not increase price or your shoppers will switch over to your competitors or stop buying the product completely. If your growth stance is RESTAGE, how can you recover profitability without increasing your price? In such a scenario, one of your alternatives is to change the size of your pack instead. Reducing the pack size, while still charging the shoppers the same price, is indirectly a price increase to the shoppers. Research has shown that shoppers are less affected with changes in pack sizes (if executed well) compared to a straightforward price increase on the product.

Imagine you are selling a 20 slice loaf of bread at £1, and are debating between either selling an 18-slice loaf of bread at £1 or selling a 20-slice loaf of bread at £1.10. Both scenarios have an effective price increase of 10% to the shopper. The shopper is likely to notice the price changes of 10p more than the fact that they are getting 2 less slices of bread in a pack. On most occasions, a shopper might not even notice the difference in pack size. Now if you are planning to reduce the bread size from 20 to 12 (-40%), that would be a noticeable difference, but the same

Get the Price Right

would be true of increasing £1 to £1.40. Pack changes are more effective if the pack size changes are marginal, and they are usually unnoticed by the shoppers. The organisation should test the principles of pack size with a sample of shoppers to identify the optimal pack size options for execution. The design of the pack is also a critical component in ensuring this tactic is implemented well. Refer to Chapter 8 for further details.

Another version of this technique is to re-frame the product completely so that the shoppers do not have the ability to do a straight price comparison between the old and the new product. Instead of selling your pack of 20 slice bread at £1, could you sell a pack of 16 at 90p instead? The comparison between the old and the new product is not that straightforward, but has the same price per bread of 5.55p as that of 18 slices at £1 or 20 slices at £1.10. You can find further examples of these on www.GetThePriceRightBook.com. In fact, if price is a key concern for the shopper, this approach has the power to increase the volume you sell as well.

Pack changes can directly or indirectly support both the GROW and RESTAGE stance across your portfolio. A reduction in pack sizes increases profitability of the product and hence supports the RESTAGE stance. On the other side, pack reduction might not directly drive an increase in your volume and revenue, but if you have planned to re-invest the improved profitability from pack changes back into driving the product harder on the shelves, it now can support your GROWTH stance. With simple modelling capability, financials assessment can be conducted to help evaluate different scenarios.

More and more organisations have adopted such practices. It is important to note that these practices, as much as it makes logical sense, might be deemed to be misleading in the eyes of the shoppers if not implemented in the right way. It is important for the organisation to ensure the value equations for the shopper still stacks up well.

KEEP THE PRICING SIMPLE

The tactics of product prices ending with 9 is nothing new, but does it work? Several research studies show that it works, and the rate at which it is being adopted has increased significantly in recent times. According to Dr Jane Price, lecturer in psychology at the University of Glamorgan, and Robert Schindler, professor of marketing at Rutgers Business School in the US, the phenomenon of 9 has the power to swing a considerable number of shoppers in their decision to buy your products. Researchers found that lowering the price of a pizza from 8.00 euros to 7.99 euros boosted sales by 15%. The answer is simply the perceived price barriers that customers may have.

Shoppers tend to put numbers in categories like 'under £5' or 'under £10' - rather than them representing a value. Shoppers tend to focus on the big denomination - which the pound sign draws the eye to - rather than the smaller denomination: the pence. There is also the emotional incentive - shoppers like to feel that they are getting better value for money.

In another experiment tested by MIT and the University of Chicago, a standard women's clothing item was tested at the prices of $34, $39, and $44. To the researchers' surprise, the item sold best at $39, even more than the cheaper $34 price! However, when tested with $40, with direct comparison with the original price, did beat the $39 in split testing. However, the number $39 still comes out on top when it is used in cohesion with a sales price.

Get the Price Right

Figure 7.3: The power of nine

Shoppers subconsciously group prices into rough price bands, and make purchasing decisions based on those parameters. Therefore a box of cereal box at $2.99 falls in the 2ish band, while another box at $3.05 falls in a 3ish band. The perception of price difference between $10 and $15 could be perceived to be smaller than that of $9.99 and $14.99. Overall results of several experiments in this field suggest that keeping the price simple and dropping it by 1c compared to your competitors could just make the difference between closing the sale, or not!

HIGH-LOW VERSUS EDLP PRICING

What pricing strategy should a retailer adopt - EDLP or Hi-Lo? This is one of the most fundamental parts of the retailer's proposition in the marketplace. Once established, it's not that easy to change overnight. Firstly let's clarify what we mean by these two terminologies. Retailers, like Wal-Mart and Aldi, that use EDLP (Every Day Low Price) maintain low prices every day and occasionally run promotions using differentiated value add pack range. EDLP retailers focus on creating a brand that consumers trust for everyday low prices on their products. EDLP retailers dominantly rely on developing a winning portfolio of own brands products. On the other hand, retailers, like Tesco, that use Hi-Lo pricing offer higher everyday prices relative to EDLP retailers. The "Lo" in Hi-Lo comes from the notion that these retailers run frequent promotions that heavily discount some products (often below EDLP). In recent times the intensity of Hi-Lo strategy has accelerated. The 'Lo' of the Hi-Lo based strategy accounting for 80% or above sale is not that abnormal.

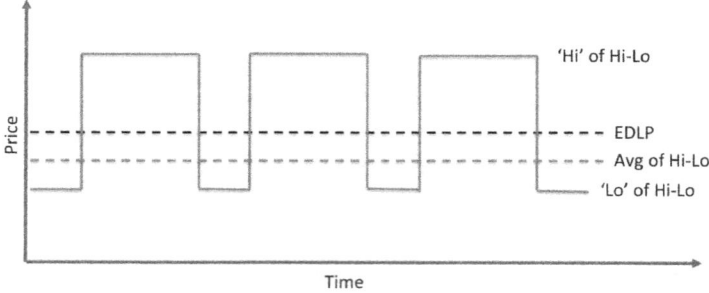

Figure 7.4: High-Low and EDLP Price

Target market for EDLP and Hi-Lo are different

Most pricing strategies clearly appeal to one category of shoppers but not to others. EDLP appeals to the more 'no-nonsense' shopper, and to simplify shopping for the time-poor/money-poor shopper, other retailers adopted a

Get the Price Right

pricing strategy whereby they charged a fair, but low-as-possible price for all products. While this is thought by some to be boring, it is very successful to this day. Hi-Lo pricing would appeal to cherry pickers - who fall into the time-rich/money-poor category. These consumers are better reached by promotional pricing strategies. Hi-Lo pricing also introduces an element of excitement into shopping - shoppers felt good when they had bought an exceptional bargain, and this would tend to encourage them to return.

So what strategy to go for? If the market is sharply segmented by cherry pickers and expected price shoppers, then the market favors a Hi-Lo strategy. If the market is dominated by time limited value driven shoppers, EDLP is the way to go. In setting your prices, you need to consider and bake in the possibility of selling your product at a deep discounted rate (e.g. 50%). If you haven't done so, the most you might be able to do is a Hi-Lo (ish) strategy which might struggle in the marketplace.

Role of manufacturers

Manufacturers have an easier role in deciding between their EDLP and Hi-Lo strategy, as they have a limited say in it. As retailers decide on their overall pricing strategy, all manufacturers can do is decide if they would like to deal with an EDLP or Hi-Lo or both types of customers. The answer to which is usually both. This is fine as long as selling to one type of retailer does not compromise the results of selling to another retailer.

Ensure pricing for EDLP versus Hi-Lo range is done fairly. There are instances where EDLP prices are lower than the 'Lo' of the Hi-Lo prices. This could potentially grow your EDLP retailer and shopper base at the expense of Hi-Lo base. If that is not what you are going for, consider a more balanced approach by a) ensuring EDLP prices are equal or slightly higher compared to your average Hi-Lo price as depicted in figure 7.4, and b) ensure the read-across of pricing is minimised between these two retail formats. The sweet spot can be identified with the support of financial modeling and shopper testing. With the rising level of technology adoption, shoppers are more informed of their choices and can compare products online before they even step into the store. Adopting a systematic and defendable channel strategy is highly recommended.

PRICE COHERENCE ACROSS YOUR PORTFOLIO

As a shopper, if a pack of 4 tissue rolls cost you £1 (with 25p each), how much do you expect to pay for the exact same pack of 10 tissue rolls? Would you expect to pay £2.50 (at 25p each), above £2.50 or below £2.50? As the key measure for the shopper in comparing these products is only the number of units, they would expect to get some level of discount of buying larger volumes (below £2.50), or at best pay an equivalent price (£2.50). Your pricing levels are defined by your organisation stance. If your 10 pack of tissue rolls has a RESTAGE stance, you would charge £2.50. If your stance is to GROW, you would charge a bit lower depending on what shoppers expect and how sustainable the financials are for it. This assumes that you are selling these products next to each other. It is possible to sell a pack of 10 tissue rolls at above £2.50 if sold in a more premium channel. Shoppers on a motorway retail outlet are likely to pay more than those buying from the city centre.

On the other hand, if the products are not directly comparable, the pricing has more flexibility. Imagine selling a plain blue t-shirt and a red t-shirt with catchy slogan printed on it. If blue t-shirt was priced at £20, would you price the red t-shirt at £20, above £20 or below £20? The answer is that it can be either of these, and is dependent on your shopper benefit matrix. If the shopper perceives the red t-shirt to be a premium compared to blue, charging above £20 is logical. However, shoppers could be indifferent to buying a blue or a red t-shirt, so having both at the same price makes more sense. Sometimes by just having the blue t-shirt next to red t-shirt can help you sell more of the reds. The shoppers get more choices and we are able to anchor the benefits of one product to another as per the 3T™ framework I had referenced earlier.

LAUNCHING A NEW PRODUCT

Launching a product is a pivotal moment because it creates expectations in your customers' minds. Once established, these create stronger associations within our mental process, and are usually more effortful to change at the later stage. Organisation is busy getting things right the first time, including pricing. With limited real life insights available on the new product, pricing can sometimes be guesswork. Of course no one knows how it is going to play out exactly after the product launch, but with our strategic review on both organisation objectives and shopper requirements in the previous chapters, setting a price for a new product becomes more targeted. It's not left to the guesswork of few individuals within the organisation.

Pricing for the new products can broadly be categorised into 3 areas – Market skimming strategy, Competitor benchmark strategy and Market penetration strategy. The figure on the next page depicts these three pricing strategies across a potential product life cycle of a product (simplified for demonstration purpose only).

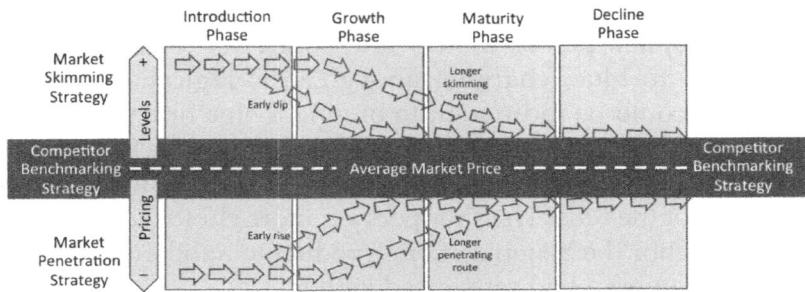

Figure 7.5: Skimming, competitive and penetration pricing strategy for new products

Market skimming pricing

Price skimming involves setting a high price before other competitors actively enter the market. The market conditions are favourable, with little or no competition, due to the product being very innovative. The current retail environment is not hugely supportive of this strategy. Even if the product is niche in its own category, products from other categories are also fighting for shoppers' attention in the store. Skimming prices here would imply just a marginal profit, enhancing prices for a very short time, before you start increasing your promotional campaign to expand your market reach and grow scale. Even if your stance is RESTAGE, the increasing competition slowly starts to dial up the attributes of the GROW stance.

Grabbing the attention of a shopper in a large retail store is very difficult, especially when you have a price hike with the product. To support the price hike, you could increase store presence by displaying your products on large displays or giving away free trials of your products. Both of these examples place emphasis on product features to enhance your value

Get the Price Right

instead of price pains. Refer to Chapter 8 for further details on how you could optimise your implementation strategies.

Referring to System 1 of the mental process, make sure you are indirectly associating your products with the right frame for your shoppers. At this stage, shoppers have limited capability of the perceived value of the product, and the initial stages of the launch are critical in shaping this going forward. If you position it rightly, skimming pricing strategy can work well, but it all boils down to how much you shout and convey about the product benefits instead of price. Instead, if you push for PRICE at the initial stage, you may get more packs being sold off the shelves in the short term but re-positioning the product at a later stage would require a lot more effort. The trick is to keep to your plan in a consistent manner, unless the market forces are just too strong to handle.

Market penetration pricing

The reverse is true for market penetration strategy as well. When a product is launched with a BIG BANG special introductory offer, it directly implies penetrating pricing strategy. This is the most widely adopted technique across the retail industry right now, as shoppers are getting more deal seekers. Penetration pricing is often used to support the launch of a new product, and works best when a product enters a market with relatively little product differentiation and where demand is price elastic – so a lower price than rival products is a competitive weapon.

Your purpose is to gain critical mass of shoppers, starting with your early adopters and more. A promotion generally triggers System 2 of the mental process, and is therefore craving for a logical explanation for the shopper to buy. This strategy aims to encourage customers to switch to the new product quicker because of the lower price. However, you are slowly training your shopper to keep buying at these low prices at a later stage. In the case where you are the first entrant in the marketplace, you happen to gain scale fast enough with low prices; soon such low prices can become the market norm. This could be good to keep competition at bay for slightly longer, but when the competition increases, a low price strategy might not be sustainable.

You can find further examples of deeply discounted promotion tactics on www.GetThePriceRightBook.com.

The recommendation with penetrating strategy is to do short bursts of promotional campaigns in early stages, and start adapting to new market dynamics sooner than later.

Achieving growth stance with pricing

Now reflecting back to our growth stance from Chapter 5, growth stance of GROW and limited product differentiated product features aligns with the principles of market penetration strategy. Growth stance of RESTAGE and differentiated product features implies going for a market skimming strategy. Competitor benchmarking strategy is simply either intending to play a balanced game or is the consequence of the organisation not being decisive on price and going with what a typical market would have priced it at. The latter is where most of the organisation takes their stance on.

All the three scenarios of these pricing techniques can be modelled to understand the implications on its internal financial and external market share. This should help in a better decision-making process; however, it's equally important to balance quantitative analysis with the qualitative version outlined earlier, or else there could be longer-term consequences.

Chapter 8
Winning at the Moment of Truth

"The great aim of education is not knowledge, but action."
- Herbert Spencer

The SPE™ framework is based on setting the foundations of having clarity on your strategic goal post based on both organisation priorities and shopper needs. Chapter 5 outlined how we translate organisation priorities across our portfolio. Chapter 6 outlined a brief approach in ensuring we understand the key shopper missions, shopper profiles and their needs, and how our products can be positioned to address those needs. Chapter 7 described key principles and tactics one could adopt in building their pricing plan.

Once this is done, this chapter tackles some of the key principles of getting your execution right and aligned to your strategic pricing. We now need to ensure that the in-store activation triggers the intended mental concept and purchasing goals in the shopper's mind. This is the third stage of the Strategic-Pricing-Execution (SPE) ™ framework, and one of the most critical ones in ensuring that all our efforts and planning delivers the results we want.

FOUR BARRIERS TO SHOPPER PURCHASE

Having a good understanding of what shoppers value in your proposition and identifying the right price is only half the battle. All your understanding of the shopper, alignment on internal objectives, clarity of your positioning in the marketplace and the pricing strategy that you are planning to deploy is just preparing you for making a lasting impact on the shoppers in the store. This is the real moment of truth, where the planning and actions of all your teams (finance, marketing, sales, supply chain etc.) across the organisation comes together when the shopper is presented with the opportunity to purchase your product on the shelves. The success is purely driven by whether the shoppers would consider your product to have the right perceived value with a fair price tag on it or not.

A recent global retail shopper study by marketing giant Ogilvy & Mather "Shopper Decisions Made In-Store" (SDMIS) revealed that 38% to 88% (dependent on different cultures and geographic regions across the globe) of shoppers make their decision in the store on what category to buy from, which brand to choose and how much they will buy. In fact, there are 4 key stages of purchasing barriers for the shoppers before they purchase a product. Only the first stage is referring to shoppers' out of store experience. The remaining stages are all focused on winning the shoppers at the moment of truth (i.e. inside the store). These four barriers are depicted in figure 8.1.

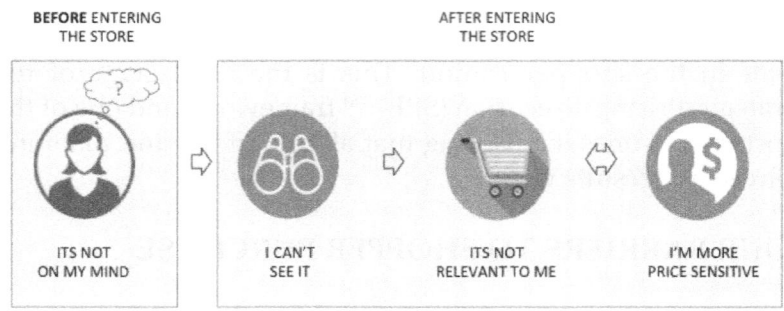

Figure 8.1: Four key stages of purchasing barriers

Get the Price Right

1. **Shoppers don't think of your product in first place** - the brand presence of your product is not strong enough. This could be because of the product lacking the required credibility and/or visibility prior to the shopper entering the retail store.

2. **Shoppers can't find your product in the store** - Even if shoppers happen to think about your product, if they cannot easily find it in the store, the sale is not made. The emergence of large display stands and big promotional banners in the retail outlets are increasingly used to enhance visibility of your products in store.

3. **Shoppers don't find your product relevant to them** – Even if the shopper happens to stumble across your product in the store, is the value proposition good enough for the shoppers to pick up your product? This could also include stocking the right pack range and sizes.

4. **Shoppers don't find your prices to be 'fair' enough** - After all the above is cleared, if the price is not reasonable, the product does not get picked up from the shelves. It is normal for shoppers to go back and forth between stage 3 and 4, and this can vary from shopper to shopper. It is also possible that a sudden encounter of price reduction on the shelves can make the shopper momentarily irrational resulting in an impulse purchase, even if the value equation doesn't stake up.

What this means is marketers must ensure they activate their brands both inside and outside of the store premises on a consistent basis, or else their shoppers will switch. Sales need to ensure they have secured the right places at a fair price for their products in the store. Operations need to ensure the execution of the plan is seamless. Finance needs to drive and support the commercials of any significant investments. These are just few examples of how cross-functional teams need to work coherently in delivering a coherent execution. In reference to leveraging pricing to enhance our chances of winning at the moment of truth, we will explore the following areas to support stages 2-4 as outlined above:

a) Get the pack right
b) Present your price in the right way
c) Location location location

GET THE PACK RIGHT

The packaging and design of your products has a big role in influencing the shopper purchase decision-making process. There are two primary intentions behind having an effective packaging – Firstly to enhance the chances of grabbing the attention of the shoppers passing through the aisle. Retail stores can be flooded with promotional campaigns, and usually stock products from a huge number of manufacturers. Fighting for shoppers' attention can be very challenging. Secondly, the right design can compliment your desired product positioning. If you are going for a premium positioning, and your product resembles an everyday standard class of product, you have missed the trick. All of a sudden your product is sending wrong signals to the shoppers, suggesting a lower perceived value. As a result the value equation might not stack up with the feel of a standard brand and the price of a premium.

It is not just a case of coming up with something you think looks great. You have to think about storage, transport, the environment and whether it fits in with retail buyers' requirements. This topic is so vast that it potentially creates a business case for me to write a whole book on it. However, in reference to pricing, let us briefly explore two key features of

Get the Price Right

packaging that can help us compliment our pricing strategy - its shape and design.

Product Shape

For instance, as shown in figure 8.2, which of the two bottles do you think can hold more?

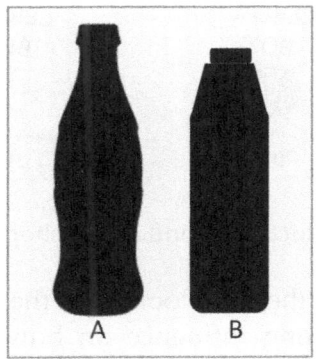

Figure 8.2 Product height influences shopper perception

Even though both of these bottles hold the same quantity, it is more likely that most of us would have said Bottle A was larger. Various studies have shown that there is a strong level of correlation between the height of the bottle and the perceived volume. If product B was your competitor with the same price (and assuming no other factors involved), shoppers are then more likely to pick up your product from the shelves.

This can be explained by how our subconscious mental processes come to this conclusion. As we have grown, more and more of us have learned to associate taller things to be bigger. So when we see a taller bottle, subconsciously we are conditioned via our system 1 of our mental process to perceive Bottle A to have more value. On a similar note, we can prioritise breadth and depth of the product. Again as shown in figure 8.3, which products would you think could hold more volume?

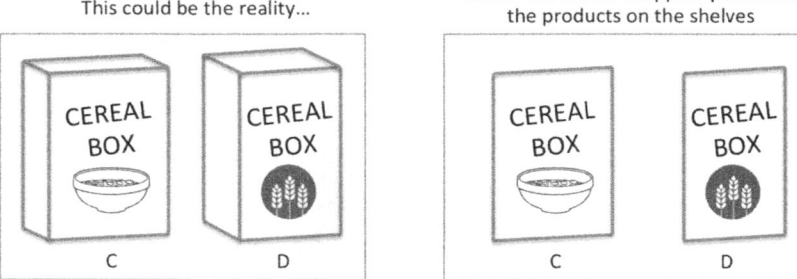

Figure 8.3 Product shape influences shopper perception

As a shopper in the store looking at the aisle, your physical visibility has a strong influence on how you intercept the product. Seeing is believing, so therefore assuming all other factors are equal, product C can appear to have more perceived value than product D.

You can leverage these tactics to support both your GROW and RESTAGE stance. If you have price-matched your competitors, your products A and C are likely to sell more. However, if you are going for a RESTAGE stance and would like to raise your prices, Bottles A and C again holds a better chance of success as shoppers are likely to have a higher value perception of these product. On a similar note, if you are considering adopting the techniques of weight out instead of increasing price (as referenced in chapter 6 under the section Pack Pack Pack), these techniques can further help minimise the risk with how your shoppers might react.

Product Design

In regard to the product packaging design, what colour themes should you use for your products? Should you be creative in doing so or play a safe game? Should we place that logo on the left or right of the pack? What picture should we use on our packaging? These are just some of the questions that one would need to consider in developing the packaging design. The key question is not how 'pretty' your product design looks, but more importantly what types of signals your shoppers receive.

As much as the designer would hate to hear, the shopper might not care about your nth level of detail embedded on the packaging. What is more important is the overall 'look and feel' of the product. Your packaging design should convey the key messages to the shoppers from even a meter or two away from the shelves. In fact, you need to make a positive impact on the shopper at such distances to create enough urges for them to at least pick up the product in the first place to explore your pretty little details on the packs.

So how does the shopper interpret the shelves from a meter or two away from it? Rory Sutherland in his book – Decoded, demonstrates a convincing point of view for it. Figure 8.4 and 8.5 shows how shoppers think they see the shelves and what actually happens.

Yes, we see things as they are, but our brain decodes and focuses on key themes from a distance.

Once the brain intercepts the 'BIG PICTURE' of your landscape, it might decide to dwell into a specific area or product on the shelf space, based on what has 'sparked' your attention. When this happens, the shelve space or specific product under focus gets clearer and the surrounding area even more blurry, as shown in figure 8.6.

Figure 8.4: What shoppers think they see

Figure 8.5: What shoppers actually see at stage 1

(For optimal results in colour, visit www.GetThePriceRightBook.com.)

Get the Price Right

Figure 8.6: Targeted visibility at stage 2

(For optimal results in colour, visit www.GetThePriceRightBook.com.)

This principle is key in designing your packaging, as we have two stages of interaction. At stage 1, our packaging needs to stand out on the shelves to seek enough of shopper's attention. At stage 2, the packaging needs to convey the right and consistent messages aligned to our targeted shopper mission and desired positioning in the marketplace. We want our product to be easily distinguishable (even within the blurry world) in contrast to our competitors. This is why some private labels are very successful in imitating their packaging style to that of a successful branded product, in the hope that a) shoppers would associate both of these products to have the similar perceived value and b) the shopper might pick up the private label instead of branded products out of confusion. Your colour theme and quality of packaging should be distinctive but also resonant with your intended communication with the shopper.

If someone were looking for healthy cereal, which colour theme would best represent this shopper mission? Would it be blackish or greenish? The one that resonates with the shopper's mission at a subconscious level, System 1 automatically prioritises these products to further focus on. For example, if you were looking to gift a premium beer bottle to your friend, which bottle would you pick for the occasion from figure 8.7?

Figure 8.7: Premium or non-premium packaging

Even if I had said that the bottle on the right is the premium one, your mental process automatically would challenge my thinking, as the bottle on the left has more natural clues of premium features.

Your packaging is your physical identify and signature of your product on the shelves, so let's make it count. Packaging has a big role in shaping how the shopper feels and perceives your product. Your packaging needs to compliment your intended shopper missions and positioning in the marketplace. By sending consistent and right messages to your shoppers, they are more likely to reward you for it.

Get the Price Right

PRESENT YOUR PRICE IN THE RIGHT WAY

The shoppers can directly locate the prices next to the product on the store shelves. As retailers, we don't have the opportunity to present our products first, get the shopper completely convinced into the purpose of the product, and then present them with the price. And in the situation when the shopper does not like the price, the retailer does not have the opportunity to further outline all the purchasing benefits again and/or end up in a price negotiation debate with the shopper.

Selling your product on shelves has some contrasting attributes to when a sales representative makes a sale. We have looked at how packaging can help in sending the right implicit signals to the shopper. Now let's look at how the presentation of price can influence the value equation for the shoppers.

Size of the price tag

Figure 8.8: Price and non-price environment

In the above example, price has been given a different level of importance based on its relative size. If we shout about the price being more important in the way we are communicating in the retail store, shoppers are also likely to give price a higher priority in their value equation. As a result, not enough focus is presented on enhancing the perceived value of the products.

There are numerous examples of this. In a supermarket, with increasing promotional push, it's all about PRICE PRICE PRICE. Whereas when you are in a Louis Vuitton store, the price tag is almost hidden way inside the product and on occasions may require a bit of search mission before one can find it. The purpose here is clearly not to focus on price too much.

Of course the global economy has a part in shaping the behaviours of the shopper to be more deal seekers, but in my opinion the bigger challenge now is how retailers have been conditioned for price to be more important in the eyes of the shoppers. There is no right or wrong answer to this. If you want to fight for shoppers with your pricing being the key marketing message, greater emphasis on price is the way to go. However, such strategies in the long run might not be profitable and sustainable.

Presentation style of the price tag

On a similar note, the styles of the price labels can also send implicit signals to the shopper on the perceived value. The figure below demonstrates how different pricing patterns could increase or decrease the value attached to it:

Figure 8.9 Price presentations influences shopper perception

The price with a shiny star would be rated more than a price on a plain white background. A flashing price would help reduce the perception of pain compared to non-flashing price. The price is always the same, but the valuation of price as pain is different due to its presentation styles. If this can influence the shopper's purchasing behaviours, it's worth baking into our consideration prior to implementing our pricing strategies.

LOCATION LOCATION LOCATION

In a busy retail environment, studies have shown that you need to convince the shopper in less than a second to be successful in getting their attention to your products. Often the decision-making process of shoppers does not occur until they actually see a product in the store. Therefore, the way a product is displayed in a store and is supported by in-store marketing materials can often be instrumental in leveraging sales. Like properties or restaurants, the new era of retail's success is dependent on getting the products in the right locations in the right way.

Effectiveness of your product displays

Merchandising effectiveness is important in understanding return on investment (ROI) for your particular products or displays. A simple financial ROI equation would compare a basic investment required for large displays versus incremental volume you sold and incremental profit you made. Of course this would give you a ballpark figure of what is working and what is not. This is good for comparing relative performance of different display types, but does not necessarily give you the true story behind the performing numbers.

A more sophisticated approach would be to really understand shopper responsiveness to your displays. Each merchandising activity needs to be assessed from multiple fronts using both internal financial and external shopper lenses to conclude on their effectiveness. To gauge a more in-depth shopper story, behind the success of the displays, I recommend focusing on three KPIs as shown in figure 8.10:

Figure 8.10: Display effectiveness shopper KPIs

The attention rate is simply the measure of the percentage of shoppers who look at a display compared to the total number of shoppers who have an opportunity to pass and see it. Out of these, the interaction rate is the percentage of shoppers who stop and actively explore the products from the displays at some levels. Out of those who interacted, the Buy – Non Buy ratio is simply the split between shoppers who end up purchasing the product versus those who didn't.

With simple well-defined shopper observation campaigns in the store, such evidence can be captured to better understand the effectiveness of the displays. Shopper habits can also be studied to understand how much of the incremental volume sold was truly incremental and what was lost opportunity to sell shoppers at full price. There are many factors that can influence the effectiveness of a display, some of which are discussed below.

Get the Price Right

Promote the right mix

The purpose of having deep promotions in the store is clear – increase store footfall, get shoppers' attention, and sell more. The better the location and visibility of the display, the stronger the expected sales performance. The location of your product can also influence how the products get positioned in the marketplace. If you have leveraged certain products to be the anchor points for your own product, or planned your portfolio to 'sandwich' price your competitors' product (as outlined in Chapter 7), being placed in the right way on the shelve is critical.

For example, a shopper is hungry and therefore is on a mission to satisfy his hunger. Your product is intended to cater for the 'hunger' mission for the shopper. Your product specification is perfect, with all the right ingredients for being an energy booster and a tasty chocolate bar. However, if your product is placed next to kid's fun style chocolate bars, it is possible for the shoppers to pick up mixed implicit signals on similarities between both chunky hungry products and fun-based children's treats.

Another recommendation is to leverage the 3T™ framework, to have a range of products at the displays – some to entice the shoppers for attention, and others to trade them up and across to more profitable range. Mixing the product range on promotions on single displays increases options for the shoppers and reduces your cost per product types per display. By shelving your product range from covering the entire display end to only half of it wouldn't necessarily half your sale.

Shoppers are used to seeing promoted products on the store's end displays, or gondolas, and will usually seek out those bargains. Be sure to place promoted products there that have a right mix of high profit margin and high attention seeker products, instead of simply the lowest price or best promotion all the time.

Display Layout and Quality

Retailers spend a lot of time and energy in making sure the store layout is planned to optimise results. You can find that products that are impulsive in nature, such as magazines and candy, are placed near the cash register or other easy to reach places. As shoppers wait to pay for their purchases, these displays may attract them to buy more, and often at a more premium price. If you are selling a pack of 200g candies at £2 in the store, you might sell a 50g pack of candy (for one-time consumption) at £1 near the cash register. There is a clear difference in price barometers between the two, but shoppers are more willing to pay a premium at the point of checkout instead of painfully skipping the line and going back to the store aisle. On the other hand, everyday essentials, such as milk and bread, could be placed in the furthest corner of the store. Shoppers must walk by other category aisles to get to the everyday essential aisles, therefore increasing the chance of these shoppers picking up additional products on their way.

The quality and types of display stands can also influence the performance of the promotion with the shoppers. Using "dump bins" or "offer bins" for close-out items can often be associated to cheap prices. On the other hand, creative display stands can increase engagement with the shopper in the store and potentially help in enhancing the perceived value of your product.

You can find further examples of various display types on www.GetThePriceRightBook.com. Explore them and get some

Get the Price Right

inspiration. I would also love to hear about what you think works when it comes to getting the displays right.

Chapter 9
With Great Pricing Power Come Great Responsibilities

"Do not exchange your dignity for popularity."
- Dr. Steve Maraboli

ETHICS – WHAT ARE YOUR LIMITS?

An organisation is under pressure to perform well, and deliver the best results it can possibly can. To what extent would one go to increase market share and profits for the organisation, before it starts to 'feel' not so right? Where is that fine line? Ethics is a very personal thing, and interpretation of it can vary from person to person. Our environment has a huge influence on what we perceive to be right or wrong. When battling with the fierce competition within the retail landscape, many organisations might be tempted to try a variety of pricing tactics to hold or grow its shopper base. Would influencing shoppers' purchasing behavior through price be unethical? In my personal opinion, as long as we are not misleading the shopper, and we are abiding by the law, the remit of pricing is in fact a key fundamental tool in developing your strategy.

As we have previously explored in Chapter 2, price is one of the key parts of the shopper's purchasing decision. To get the value equation for the shopper in the favor of the organisation, you need to get the right balance between the perceived value and the price of the product. Price is a very powerful tool in conveying key messages to your shoppers. With such heavy reliance on price, how can an organisation not leverage it to keep the shoppers well informed? After all, if the shoppers believe the price is not right, they will simply not buy your products, and vice versa. An organisation cannot afford to not understand their shopper's needs and how price can communicate the true value of the product. If the shoppers want a decent quality product at an affordable price, you give that to them. If the shoppers are happy to pay a premium for a product with added features and benefits, you give that to them. Your role is to ensure the shoppers are getting an adequate quality and experience, in line with your commitment (verbally and visually) to them.

From a commercial point of view, if you don't leverage price in the right way, your competitors might. In doing so, if you happen to run out of business, and your competitors monopolise the market, it surely can't be good for the shoppers. Organisations don't have to be over-generous to their shoppers to prove that they have strong ethical values. On the other hand, if they price it too high, shoppers will respond by not buying the product. Ethics is a very personal thing, and you should decide what you deem to be right and not so right.

REGULATIONS

A legal aspect of pricing is more straightforward than ethics. It is usually (or at least should be) black and white in the way it is interpreted by everyone to be what is right or wrong. This section is not a legal advice, and you should consult your own legal solicitor if in doubt on any legal matters. My intention is to raise some awareness for retailers and manufacturers to take pricing practices very seriously and conduct it within the parameters of the law. There are several laws across the globe about the way pricing is governed. For our purpose at hand, there are two key aspects of particular importance for pricing.

Firstly, pricing should not be misleading to shoppers and, secondly, pricing should abide by the governing competitive law.

Misleading shoppers with pricing is becoming a trend

Retailers could face legal action for misleading shoppers with dodgy promotions, shrinking products and confusing unit prices showcased to the shoppers. According to WhickUK? magazine, there are hundreds of misleading offers on the shelves every day that do not comply with the rules. Their investigation and analysis on UK supermarket comparison found that promotions such as 'was/now' offers, where a product is on sale at a discounted price for longer than the higher price applied, were misleading. For example, promoting new toothpaste at £2, when the base price at £3, was only offered for 21 days. Additional examples of unlawful pricing practices include:

- Increasing the price of products prior to the launch of a volume promotion. This is especially relevant to multi-buys promotions
- Advertising special offers just to bring in shoppers when you do not really expect to be able to supply the products (so-called bait advertising)
- Pretending that an offer is only available for a very limited time to pressure customers into an immediate decision. Really is that how desperate organisations have become?!
- Falsely claiming accreditation - for example, claiming to be registered under an accreditation scheme when you are not
- Intentionally developing complexity in unit prices to discourage shoppers from comparing prices between products. For example, making cross read between competitor products difficult by stating one in per 100ml and the other in per 100g.

- And so on…

> For a special report on misleading prices and real life examples of unlawful pricing practice, visit www.GetThePriceRightBook.com.

Consumers should never be misled, and it should always be clear what they are getting for the price. Such practices are only going to raise more and more shopper complaints. If this doesn't get addressed as soon as possible, relevant retailers may face hefty penalties, along with potential loss of their credibility and trust with their shoppers.

Competitive act exists for a reason

Are you really allowed to charge whatever price you like for your products? In general, you are free to set prices, as long as it is not used in an anti-competitive manner. Predatory pricing tactics is a classic example of such, whereby you deliberately underprice your product to drive competitors out of business and/or discourage new competitors. On another hand, you must also not conspire with competitors to fix prices in a cartel.

For manufacturers, setting a recommended retail price (RRP) is little complex in nature. Controlling the price retailers (who stock manufacturers' products to sell) charge for the product is against competition law. One is not allowed to exert direct or indirect pressure on retailers. If you feel that you need to set a recommended price, you should take advice on how you can ensure that you are not breaching competition law.

I would strongly recommend for you and your organisation to follow an ethical and lawful pricing practice. If your organisation wants to drive market share and/or profitability in a coherent manner, I encourage you to review and adopt some of the powerful pricing techniques outlined in this book, that allow you to grow profitably in the right way.

About the Author

Sahaj Kothari
Mr. Get the Price Right

Strategist | Entrepreneur | Author

Sahaj Kothari, the Pricing and Growth Sage, is a serial Strategy Consultant who has helped businesses big and small turn around their performance by embedding powerful pricing and growth strategies. He is the founder of Ensere consulting, and brings over a decade of first hand experience from multiple industries such as FMCG, Retail, Technology, Telecom and more. He breaks the traditional mould of doing things, which might seem to work on paper, and believes in delivering a lasting legacy in an invigorating manner.

Sahaj has a vision to make our Retail experience more refreshing, engaging and progressive. GET THE PRICE RIGHT is one of the many steps towards this vision, and Sahaj would love to connect with you to make it a reality.

www.sahajkothari.com | www.getthepricerightbook.com | www.ensere.com

Connect @sahajkothari

Lightning Source UK Ltd.
Milton Keynes UK
UKOW06f1511300915

259588UK00003B/3/P